Step Up, Step Out

A GIRL'S GUIDE TO EMPOWERMENT, SELF-LEADERSHIP AND SUCCESS

by Daphne Wallbridge

DaphneWallbridge

Step Up, Step Out
A Girl's Guide to Empowerment, Self-Leadership, And Sucess

Print ISBN: 978-1-48358-894-0
eBook ISBN: 978-1-48358-895-7

To my daughter, Phoebe. May you always have the courage and grit to go after your dreams and ambitions, but most of all, enjoy the journey that will get you there.

— Your Mama, xoxo

Table of Contents

Introduction

Whether you have just graduated and are starting off your career, or have just landed a promotion, you are embarking on a new and exciting journey. You are undoubtedly enthusiastic and at the same time, nervous that change is just around the corner. You ask yourself if you made the right move, if you will be able to do the job, if you have made the right choice. All of these questions and doubts are natural and are manageable—with the right tools. This is why I wrote *Step Up, Step Out*: To help women everywhere face the challenges that come with managing careers as well as professional transitions.

The Beginning

I still remember how it all started. My husband David came home one day and started talking about an interesting radio host who was on the air. This man was hosting a session on Sirius's Springsteen channel. The host, Stewart Friedman, was a professor at the Wharton School of Business who happened to be a huge Springsteen fan. As Friedman captivated his audience, he also referred to his new book entitled *Leading the Life You Want*. Suffice it to say, David was curious and purchased a copy. Friedman's book highlights six formidable and varied leaders, Bruce Springsteen being one of them, Sheryl Sandberg being another. As David began reading about Sandberg, he decided to research her. He found her TED Talk and quickly called me over to watch it with him. I was hooked! I knew right there and then that I had found my calling, my passion, and my purpose. I wanted to focus on women's leadership issues. I also wanted to have my voice heard and make a difference.

That's when it hit me. Sandberg struck a chord with me when she explained why there are so few women leaders. She discussed the challenges women face in the workforce and the realities of climbing the ladder while balancing work and family. Being the mother of a toddler at the time, I was hearing her loud and clear. Although I had a wonderfully supportive husband, I was still struggling to find my voice, my path, and my purpose. Sandberg's talk fixed that! I now knew where I was heading. Soon after, I read her book, *Lean In*, as well as several other great feminist manifestos. After that, I became inspired to write, and I started Step Up, an informative blog devoted to women's leadership issues.

Having been a high school teacher for the last 15 years, and now a new high school vice principal, I knew firsthand how much guidance young women needed. I knew they loved the idea of leaving home and making it on their own, but often had absolutely no idea what was ahead of them—no clue! I know this for a fact because I was in the same boat, along with many others.

As time passed, I found that I became increasingly interested in leadership. I loved working with people. I loved helping people solve problems. And I loved leading teams. More specifically, I also began developing an interest in empowering the young women I came across every day. In 2015 I started 20/20 Horizons, a young women's leadership program in the high school where I taught at the time. There, I attempted to address important issues and topics—such as communication, building strong networks, managing personal finances, and setting goals—that would serve young women well in life as they transitioned from home to the real world. My ultimate goal, however, would be to host a 20/20 Horizons day, where young girls from my community can enroll and spend the day being uplifted, empowered, and guided through interesting, meaningful activities and guest speakers. In the meantime, however, I have chosen to expand 20/20 Horizons on a more global level with the help of Facebook. There, young women from across the world can join in on interesting and empowering conversations. In fact, I have received some inspirational personal messages from girls living in impoverished areas of the world telling me how meaningful the forum has been to them! To join this forum, simply go to www.facebook.com/horizons2020/ .

Step Up and Step Out encompasses the key lessons I share with the young women I meet. It's meant to be used as a guidebook or an instruction manual, if you will, for life's challenges. In this book, I offer advice and tips on how you can find your voice, develop your mind, and move toward a path that will bring you joy and personal fulfillment—no matter where you are in your career. Given the myriad challenges of today's fast-paced world, this is not an easy task. However, I firmly believe that if you are equipped with the proper tools—knowledge, confidence, and a personal vision—then, you have a leg up.

As I was starting this book, I kept asking myself just how I wanted to address today's young women. The answer came to me as I was reading a great book entitled *Nice Girls Don't Get the Corner Office* by Dr. Lois Frankel. As I started reading Frankel's book, I noticed that it was divided into small manageable sections that related to common mistakes women made in their careers: 133 to be precise! What I also liked about her book was that after each mistake mentioned, Frankel offered coaching tips to address them. I loved that model and, thus, decided to center my book around this approach.

This book is intended as a guide or a how-to book and is designed for reference when needed. You can read it from start to finish or digest each lesson and then move on to the next—it's really up to you!

Lastly, as I reflect on the lessons offered in this book, I foresee a time when I will be guiding my own daughter, Phoebe, in her professional journey as well as in life. This book is also my gift to her—my words of wisdom, if you will. Therefore, I present the best lessons I've learned throughout my readings and leadership experience. I've picked and chosen relevant lessons I find critically important for today's professional women as they move forward in their careers. After each lesson, I offer <u>Step Up Doables,</u> concrete steps women can take to move ahead, take control, and ultimately become the architects of their future.

This is my wish for you, and it is the reason I wrote this book. These are exciting times, and they will offer you a chance to take charge of your dreams, act on them, and carve out your unique path.

Now, let's Step Up and Step Out!

Daphne

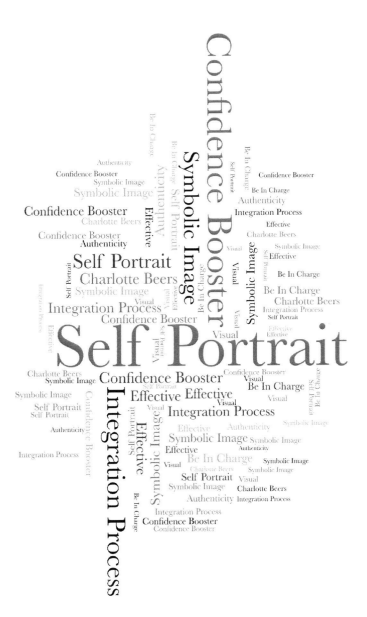

Lesson 1: The Self Portrait

"Your portrait allows the wisdom and wishes of your heart to infuse and then magnify the intellectual, high-performance side of you."

– Charlotte Beers, American Business Woman

I wanted to start off this book with the self-portrait. By self-portrait, I'm not referring to the typical portrait where you have your photo taken or sit for an artist for hours on end. This self-portrait is much more meaningful than that and has at its core the purpose of guiding you along your path to self-cultivation and personal growth. Intrigued? Curious to see exactly how this works? Well, let me give you more detail and then let's get to work!

I first read about the concept of the self-portrait from Charlotte Beers, author of *I'd Rather Be in Charge*. The idea is simple and effective. Here's how it works. A symbolic self-portrait is an image you conjure up in your mind that represents you, your strengths, and the person you want to become. It's an activity that involves delving deep into your background and analyzing your life. You must consider your family history, traditions, relationships, and education—everything that has helped shape the person you are today. Beers describes this to be an <u>integration process,</u> where one puts the various pieces of the puzzle together to try and find a meaningful symbol. In the end, the purpose of the activity is to have the image of the symbol crystallize in your mind to help you embody the person you want to become.

There is no perfect recipe for creating a self-portrait. In her book, Beers suggests doing this activity in two phases. The first phase occurs before the self-portrait (who you are now); the second is the actual choosing of an image to be your *figurative* self-portrait (who you want to become).

In this book, I have opted to focus on the <u>after</u> self-portrait, the symbolic image that represents the <u>ideal you</u>. I have applied this approach in my professional setting and found it to be very powerful in challenging situations.

The Tea Bag

To help further explain the concept of the self-portrait, I thought I would offer my own example: the tea bag!

Before choosing my own symbolic self-portrait, I had some thinking and reflection to do. I had to dig deep into who I wanted to be and sum up the essential qualities I wanted to embody in both my personal and professional lives. I came up with the following qualities: strength, courage, openness, resilience, and grit.

I've always loved the quote by Eleanor Roosevelt: "A woman is like a tea bag; you never know how strong it is until it's in hot water."

I try to adhere to this philosophy every day because I'm often in situations where the emotions are intense and the pressure is on. The more I progress in my career, the more stress comes my way. Often, I need to be on my feet, make decisions, and move on. Given the pace of my work, it's not always easy to remain calm and in control.

When these types of situations arise, I take time to breathe (very important; never forget to breathe) and then I visualize the image of my tea bag going into hot water. I tell myself, "that's me!" I can be soothing and calm (like a nice cup of tea). However, when the pressure is on (the boiling water) my strength comes out (the tea)—I perform and step up to the plate.

In the end, the image helps me re-center and regain my composure. It helps wipe away all the white noise that surrounds me and acts as my personal pillar of strength. As simple as it sounds, it's one of the most powerful tools I have in my empowerment toolkit. Because it is so effective, I make sure to keep my symbolic portrait nearby as a constant reminder. I love visual reminders, so I keep an image of a tea bag being submerged in hot water as a screen saver. Every time I open my iPad, I remind myself of my portrait and it gives me a subtle psychological boost. What's more, I also have the tea bag image framed in my office with Eleanor Roosevelt's quote! I keep it at my desk as a subtle and constant reminder that I can handle any challenge that comes my way.

STEP UP DOABLES

- Read *I'd Rather Be in Charge* by Charlotte Beers.
- Start journaling every day. This is the best way to get to know the <u>real you</u>, get in touch with your emotions, and eventually find that self-portrait. As you write down your thoughts and ideas, you clear your head and make room for other important thoughts. Furthermore, you save energy and refocus on what's important. It's also a great way to have an internal dialogue, set goals, and refocus on

priorities. For this activity, you can use a traditional paper journal or go high tech and get a great journaling app—I like My Wonderful Days because it is compatible with my MacBook and syncs with my iPad. It is also simple to use and allows you to go back in time. There are lots of other options available, though; you simply need to see what e-journal works best for you.

- Once you visualize your self-portrait, search for a representative image and post that image somewhere nearby so that you can see it regularly and use it as a tool to harness strength and courage.

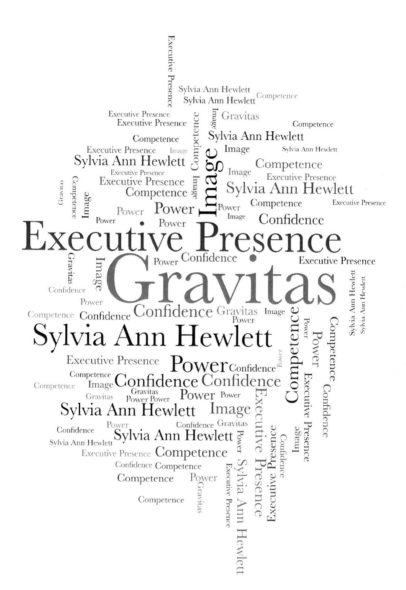

Lesson 2: Build Gravitas

"Gravitas, according to 62 percent of the leaders we surveyed, is what signals to the world you're made of the right stuff and can be entrusted with serious responsibility."

– Sylvia Ann Hewlett, Economist

Have you ever noticed how some people have a way of making you feel at ease? You know instinctively that you are in good hands. Why is that? What do these people do that reassures you? One word: gravitas. In *Executive Presence*, expert Dr. Sylvia-Ann Hewlett, explains that *gravitas* is "an amalgam of qualities that telegraphs to the world that you are in charge or deserve to be." She also quickly points out that "It's a measure of image: Whether you signal to others that you have what it takes, that you're star material" (pp. 15–16).

So, if you are not familiar with gravitas, it's time you get to know it well. This should be in every professional woman's vocabulary and in the back of her mind as she proceeds in her career. Why? Because people are watching you, evaluating you, and sizing you up at every chance they get. What's more, during an extensive study conducted with 268 senior executives, Hewlett discovered that 67% of CEOs interviewed preferred, above all else, employees that demonstrated gravitas. In other words, Hewlett's research indicated that executives favor confident employees who are competent in their field and who can delve deeper into their topics, if necessary, to get their point across.

Key elements to achieving gravitas include competence, specialized knowledge, and the ability to communicate and present oneself well. Ultimately, employers want someone who will stand tall, defend her point of view with credible sources and insight, and go to the wall to move her team toward progress and innovation. They want a leader who will naturally draw a productive entourage.

As you move forward in your career, keep the notion of gravitas in mind and remember the basics:

- Focus on what you know—your area of specialty
- Display confidence at all times
- Communicate clearly and efficiently
- Polish your appearance

STEP UP DOABLES

- Read *Executive Presence* by Sylvia Ann Hewlett.
- Mind your posture and appearance to exude professionalism and composure.
- Be generous with credit. Since great achievements rarely happen in isolation, make sure not to hog the spotlight. When you properly credit your teammates, this highlights your willingness to underscore others' talent and contribution, which is excellent for building credibility, a strong reputation as a formidable leader, and gravitas.
- Focus on your expertise. People will know if you are treading on thin ice. Stick to your area of specialization by backing your statements with credible sources and examples. Also, be willing to acknowledge any shortcomings;

people will respect you for being authentic and willing to refer to other specialists to offer the best results.

- Show humanity. Never forget that you are working with human beings. People have feelings and a life outside of work, so be sensitive to people's needs. Do not be afraid to admit mistakes, and remain transparent and humble. This will help build your gravitas because people will be naturally drawn to your willingness to be open.

- Smile more. As simple as this may be, smiling projects the image of a confident and happy person. As a result, this attracts positive attention and helps foster dynamic group work. People will be drawn to you because you project likeability.

- Empower others. By uplifting members of your team, you will inadvertently be seen as a transformational leader and someone whose focus is on the bigger picture. This is the best way to harness talent and assemble a diverse and solid team. In doing so, your gravitas will grow and you will be seen as a mobilizer, a builder, and an agent of change.

- Snatch victory from the jaws of defeat. Don't forget to keep reinventing yourself. Learn and grow from your mistakes. They are life's best lessons! Stay fresh, stay hungry, and stay curious. See all setbacks as opportunities to discover something new and meaningful.

- Drive change rather than be changed. Identify what needs work and take action. Don't fall victim to circumstance. Instead, assemble a focused group and address the situation head on with passion and positive energy.

Lesson 3: Learn The Power Of Body Language

"We convince by our presence, and to convince others we need to convince ourselves."

– Amy Cuddy, American Social Psychologist

Learning to communicate well will become one of your best assets. Social scientists talk about two main forms of communication: verbal and nonverbal. This lesson will focus on the power of nonverbal communication, better known as *body language*. Dr. Albert Mehrabian, renowned psychology professor at UCLA, observed that body language accounts for more than half of your credibility; I thought it would be a great topic for this lesson. After all, being able to communicate your message and present yourself to the world is necessary if you are going to be heard and lead change.

Nonverbal Communication

Did you know that only 7% of what you say is actually being heard? According to Mehrabian, the magic formula is as follows: When you speak, 7% of your message relates to *what* you say, your content, 38% of your message relates to *how* you say it (the sound of your voice), and 55% of your message relates to your body language—the way you move and present yourself, the way you look. In other words, your content is not worth much compared to how you convey your message. Knowing this, it only makes sense to take a closer look at the power of developing good body language skills.

Playing High and Playing Low With Body Language

According to social psychologist Deborah Gruenfeld, "People are going to decide if you are competent or not in less than one hundred milliseconds—and then it's over." That's a pretty harsh statement; nonetheless, it is true. Knowing this, it is important to tap into the power of proper body language as soon as you meet someone. Gruenfeld explains that there are two ways to present body language: You can either play high or play low. What's more, she stresses knowing when to use these poses as your greatest advantage—the key to making a powerful impact as a communicator.

Playing High

According to Gruenfeld, "playing high" means physically expanding your body to take up as much room as possible. Gruenfeld notes that a person who plays high is often in a state of total relaxation and feels as if people are watching over her, making sure she is safe. She is at the top and feeling great. As she walks, people move out of the way. When communicating, she keeps her head still, avoids all jerky movements, and holds eye contact for a few seconds longer—3 to 5 seconds. By contrast, when others are addressing her (lower positioned people), she tends to look elsewhere and break eye contact. Because, hey, she has better things to do, right?

Though this can be an effective way of communicating your point, Gruenfeld cautions us to be mindful when playing high and adopting high-power body language. She notes that it should never be used when speaking to someone who is higher ranked than you are, but rather, when you <u>want to reinforce your own rank</u> or <u>when you're in competition and status is up for grabs</u>. Otherwise, you could be sending the message that you are disconnected, detached, and not mindful of others—not the qualities a good leader wants to embody.

Playing Low

Contrary to playing high, "playing low" entails diminishing your appearance and your footprint. When playing low, people physically close themselves off by crossing their arms or touching their face or mouth. In other words, they seek to protect themselves and hide. They look elsewhere and avoid eye contact, except when they glance quickly to check for approval.

Gruenfeld highlights the advantages of playing low when a high-status person tries to relate to and connect with those with lower status. In this situation, Gruenfeld explains that playing low can actually become an asset for the high-status person, as playing low enables high-powered people to break down boundaries that impede progress and collaboration. Accordingly, there are two reasons a high-status person would play low: (a) to make herself feel comfortable, and (b) to make the other person feel comfortable.

Gruenfeld also stresses that women are <u>socialized</u> to play low and adopt low power poses. Knowing this, it is essential for women to be aware of what messages they are sending as they communicate and make the necessary adjustments.

Our Body Language Shapes Who We Are and Who We Become

A lot of interesting research has been conducted over the past years on the topic of nonverbal communication. One study, in particular, conducted by Harvard Business Professor Dr. Amy Cuddy and colleagues, revealed that the body language we use can help shape our attitude and perceptions, as well as enhance our confidence levels.

Cuddy's study suggests that by adopting various poses—whether high power or low power—it is possible to alter testosterone and cortisol levels in the body. When done properly, high-power poses can increase one's confidence (raise testosterone levels) and decrease stress (lower cortisol levels).

Examples of High-Power Poses

1. Hands on the hips with legs slightly spread out past the shoulders.

2. Leaning over a table with arms spread out parallel to the shoulders.

3. Sitting in a chair, leaning back with hands behind the head.

Examples of Low-Power Poses

1. Crossing your arms across your chest and hunching forward.

2. Placing your hand on your neck as if to protect it.

3. Crossing your legs and tucking them under your chair.

In her experiment, Cuddy had several participants adopt power poses. After two minutes of holding the power pose, saliva tests indicated an <u>increase in testosterone and a decrease in cortisol</u>. The opposite was true for the participants who adopted low-power poses for the required two minutes. In other words, the low-power pose group saw their testosterone levels decrease and their cortisol levels increase.

As women, we need to be mindful of this, since we are socialized to take on low-power poses without even knowing it—as previously mentioned by Deborah Gruenfeld. However, thanks to Cuddy's research, it is possible to be alert and watch for indications that we are sending the wrong message to others, but more importantly to ourselves.

STEP UP DOABLES

- Watch Amy Cuddy's TED talk: Your Body Language Shapes Who You Are.
- Watch Deborah Gruenfeld's lecture (found in the *Lean In* "Education" series), "Power and Influence."
- Read Amy Cuddy's book, *Presence: Bringing Your Boldest Self to Your Biggest Challenges*.
- Before going into a meeting, take a minute to think about how you will sit, stand, talk, and look at the other person. Go back to that list when you are in your meeting and adjust your presence accordingly.

- Practice power posing a few minutes before a stressful event. Find a discrete place (like a bathroom stall) and strike that power pose!

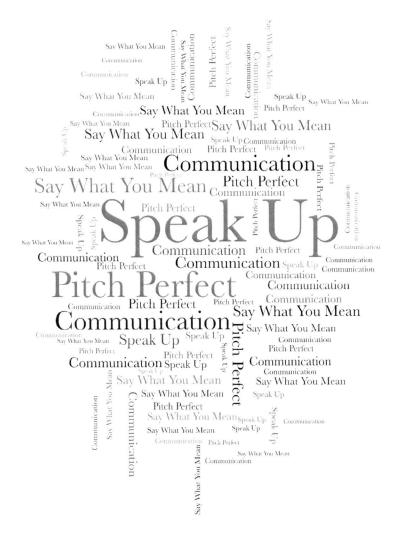

Lesson 4: It's Not What You Say, It's How You Say It

"I've learned that people will forget what you said, people will forget what you did, but people will never forget how you made them feel."

– Maya Angelou, American Poet

As previously mentioned, the way we speak (how you sound) bears a lot of weight on being heard—in fact, 38% according to Dr. Albert Mehrabian. Knowing this, it is wise to arm yourself with the proper tools that will help you convey your message clearly, concisely, and economically.

The following tips come from three well known authors: Dr. Lois Frankel, author of *Nice Girls Don't Get the Corner Office*, Dr. Sylvia Ann Hewlett, author of *Executive Presence*, and Charlotte Beers, author of *I'd Rather Be in Charge*. All three women clearly explain the essence and key elements needed to properly convey messages.

Say What You Mean and Mean What You Say

Often, women tend to express a statement with a question to <u>soften</u> their impact. It normally sounds like this:

"Maybe we should try to review the monthly budget on a set schedule to ensure that matters are dealt with more efficiently?"

Starting a statement with "maybe" and ending it with a question diminishes its importance and takes away value. It also signals to others that there is doubt or insecurity about your idea. Instead, it's much more effective to state what you want clearly and directly in a normal tone—minus the ambiguous tone and lingering question.

"I believe it would be best to review the monthly budget on a set schedule. This would ensure that matters are dealt with efficiently. I'd love to get your input on this idea."

Not only is this approach more effective and professional, it also signals to others that you value group work and the opinions of others.

Stop Over-Explaining

According to Frankel, women are often guilty of over-explaining, since they feel that getting to the point and stopping there makes them appear too authoritative and pushy. They've made their point, but somehow they have this uncontrollable urge to keep talking. Brevity and parsimony are essential to boosting one's presence and gravitas; that's why it's best to stop talking. When people over-explain and fill every moment with talk, the audience eventually checks out. The results? Both your credibility and status decline.

Slow Down and Breathe

The habit of talking too fast is another mistake women often make. Frankel explains that not only do audiences strain to understand the message, but they may also feel slightly irritated given the speed at which they're forced to take in a large amount of information. In light of this, it is critical to keep your audience's needs in mind. Make sure they can hear you and give them the opportunity to consolidate the information being provided. Remember, nothing screams out insecurity and nervousness more than rapid speech. Slow down, take a breath, and enjoy your moment. You have the right to be there and be heard.

Pitch Perfect

Have you ever noticed how some people's voices tend to go up an octave when they get nervous? Unfortunately, this is often particularly true for women. If you are one of those women, Frankel cautions us to watch out for it. Just like speaking too quickly, high-pitched voices are associated with insecurity and nervousness. Furthermore, studies have shown that people with high-pitched voices are perceived as less credible and less powerful, whereas those with low-pitched voices are seen as more powerful and in control. With that in mind, listen to yourself as you talk to people, particularly in stressful situations. If you hear your voice go up an octave, pause and adjust. This practice will make a world of difference and will send the message to others that you are calm, confident, and in control.

Know the Lingo

Whether you're starting off in an organization or have been there for the past fifteen years, you must know the workplace lingo. Basically, "workplace lingo" is the technical vocabulary used in an organization among personnel. Get to know the lingo at your workplace and make use of it in your daily conversations at work. There is nothing more discrediting to a person's image than someone who is verbally fumbling and searching for her words.

Speak Up! I Can't Hear You

If you have an important message to say, speak louder. Again, you don't want audience members to be wasting their energy trying to listen to you when they could be leaning back in their chairs enjoying your message. What's more, soft-spoken people are seen as powerless, weak, and lacking confidence. Instead, raise your voice so that the furthest person in the room can easily hear you. The added benefit to doing this is that when you do speak up, your posture automatically adjusts itself, giving you the look of someone who is in control and confident—bonus points for building credibility and gravitas!

Learn to Hang-Up

Who hasn't been guilty of this? Have you ever caught yourself leaving a long, rambling phone message? I have, and this is another power buster. There is nothing more frustrating than being held hostage by your telephone, listening to a never-ending message. Instead, keep it brief, articulate, and leave enough information to make your point. Then, hang up. Many women feel that leaving a shorter more direct phone message is a harsher approach. According to Frankel, they fear being perceived as cold and detached, which is why they like to fill the air time. This is akin to over-explaining a point, as previously mentioned, when in actuality, no one is interested in hearing a long-winded telephone message. Their time is precious as well. Keep it brief and hang up, but don't forget to address what the call is about, especially if it is important. This way, the other person can prepare accordingly for the conversation. After all, you only want to convey the essentials so you can have a more detailed conversation later on, no? When your message is too long, too wishy-washy, or too vague, you lose credibility and the receiver of your message may not detect the urgency or importance behind your reason for calling.

It's What They Hear

Charlotte Beers states it so well when she says "It's what they <u>hear</u>, not what you <u>say</u>!" In effect, you may know what you want to say, but does your audience get the same message? Remember that communication is not only conveying information; it's also the art of inspiring, motivating, and engaging an audience. Keep this in mind when presenting in front of a group. Make sure to evaluate each word you use in light of what you are trying to say. Does your message align with your vocabulary, visual, and audio support? Words have a big impact; choose them wisely.

Be Human

People want to relate to a human being, not a robot or the illusion of a perfect person. Open yourself up to your audience and let them in. A little bit of vulnerability can go a long way in engaging people and acquiring followers. I'm not telling you to divulge your family's deepest, darkest secrets, but rather, something that is appropriate for the occasion and that will give your audience pause. Initially, you sometimes need to make it about you to eventually make it about them. Humanizing yourself is key to fostering loyalty and trust.

Remember, You're Always On: Consistency Matters

This last tip is very important. You'll notice a common thread throughout this book: consistency. In this case, Beers stresses the importance of being consistent when communicating or speaking is realizing that you're always being evaluated, whether by e-mail, telephone, or even when saying hello to someone in an elevator. Whether you like it or not, people are assessing your level of power and authority by the way you sound—all the time. Be mindful of how you present yourself to the world, even with your friends and family. Use proper vocabulary and grammar. Practicing proper communication techniques in more relaxed settings will undoubtedly prepare you for more intense moments when you really need to be on.

STEP UP DOABLES

- Read *The Credibility Code* by Cara Hale Alter, a wonderful and practical book on mastering the art of public speaking.

- Before going into your boss's office to discuss specific matters, make a list of items you want to address, and write down key words you want to use. This will help you organize your thoughts and ensure you get to the point.

- When talking in front of a group, ask a friend or trusted colleague to give you feedback on your performance. Ask her to focus on certain aspects such as pitch, speed of talk, and eye contact.

- Before a presentation, practice, practice, practice! You want to make sure you know your stuff like the back of your hand. The better prepared you are, the better you'll sound.

- Before a big meeting or a presentation, practice two minutes of high-power poses (see Lesson 3). Take the time to isolate yourself and get into a positive and strong frame of mind. This will help you exude confidence and presence.

- Read Chapter 4 in Dr. Frankel's book, *See Jane Lead* on "headline communication."

- Watch *Own the Room* by Bill Hoogterp. You can find it in the Lean In website under "Education." He offers great advice on nailing public speaking.

Lesson 5: Be Financially Independent

"The way to build your savings is by spending less each month."

– *Suze Orman, American Author and Financial Advisor*

As I was researching this book, I came across some interesting articles and books discussing the advantages of being a young, financially independent woman. Of course, I believe the main reasons are obvious, but they do bear repeating. This lesson focuses on these important reasons and takes a closer look at why women should be setting aside, on a regular basis, a little something for themselves.

What Money Can Do for You

No matter how old you are or what you do in life, being financially independent allows you to have a greater sense of control and more decision-making power. Furthermore, financial security offers a sense of personal liberty, enables you to live your life on your own terms, and allows you to pursue your dreams. In fact, many women, including young professionals starting off as well as middle-aged women set in their careers, have stated that financial freedom lets them take a stand, have their voices heard, and, as a result, increase their self-confidence and sense of self-worth.

The art and science of investing can be simple: Spend less on frivolities, and save more! Okay, I know, this is a bit too simplistic and often very challenging, given all the easily accessible tempting items out there (thank you, online shopping!), but it is the simplest and most effective way of saving money! Since this is key in growing your net worth and ensuring personal financial freedom, let's explore this concept closer. The following section is divided in to four steps that must be addressed in the order presented. They are general and effective guidelines in helping women master their finances and chart a path toward personal financial freedom.

Step 1: Get to Know the Financial YOU

According to financial expert and author Carl Richards, the first questions you must ask yourself are:

1. Why is money important for me?
2. What are my values related to money?
3. What goals should I set for myself that remain true to my needs and values?

The answers to these questions will vary according to your desired lifestyle and personal values. It is important to do the initial ground work to find out what it is exactly you want out of money. Once you figure out the answers to these important questions, you are well on your way, since knowing *why* money is important to you will enable you chart to a path that will align with your ultimate financial vision.

Step 2: Do the Math

Once you've figured out why it is you want to be financially independent, you need to figure out your net worth. To do this, Richards suggests the following exercise. Divide a piece of paper in two and write down on one side all of your assets (e.g., savings, properties, investments) and on the other, your liabilities (e.g., monthly payments, outstanding debts). Lastly, subtract your total liabilities from your total assets. That number will give you your net worth. Your net worth is important and will be the starting point of your financial plan. Keep that number close by.

Step 3: Prioritize

Let's say that your calculations have made you realize that you need to pay off a total of $5,000 in outstanding debt. You have a few options at this point.

1. Pay off the highest interest debt first (often credit cards can charge up to 18% or 19% interest!), and

2. Meet with a banker and consolidate your debts into one monthly payment. This last option will simplify the payment process and may allow you to tackle your debt at a lower interest rate.

While the debt is being addressed, you must also make room for savings. The goal here is to start—no matter how much you put in your savings account—just start with something. Tony Robbins, world-renowned financial guru, explains that it is critical to stop focusing on short-term visions, and rather, focus on your *future self.* He also recommends focusing on the power of compounding interest, where the money works for you. He offers the following example. Let's say you save $1,000 at 10% interest. In one year, that initial $1,000 investment will have grown into $1,100. You will have made $100 without lifting a finger. What's more, now, your initial investment will work even harder by generating more money from $1,100 to $1,210 the following year. Get the picture?

Step 4: Diversify

This last section will vary according to your comfort zone. Some people are happy being a little riskier with their savings, while others prefer to play it safe. No matter where you fall in this spectrum, there is always a bit of room to diversity. The key lesson here is to aim for some balance. As such, Robbins recommends using "buckets" to help you diversify your portfolio. Here's how that works.

Bucket 1: Security. This first bucket should be your safety bucket. Here, you should place roughly 55% of your savings into **safe** investments such as bonds, or other forms of guaranteed savings.

Bucket 2: Growth. In this second bucket, you will want to place your money in riskier investments—such as stocks—that may yield bigger profits. Here, the recommendation is 30%.

Bucket 3: Dream. This last bucket is where you would put money made from other investments. Its ultimate purpose is to improve your lifestyle. The recommendation for this is bucket is 15% of your profits. A good option for this could be investing 7.5% in gold and 7.5% commodities.

Once more, these are only recommendations brought forth by financial experts. Ultimately, the decision is very personal. One person may wish to only focus on Buckets 1 and 2, while another may simply focus on Bucket 1. Every situation is unique and requires research and consultation to make a sound financial decision that truly reflects your needs and values.

As a final thought: What's truly important is to start where you are and work from there. It is never too early or too late. Ask yourself the important questions, get to know your net worth, pay off debt while setting up a savings plan, and diversify.

STEP UP DOABLES

- Set up an external savings account that you cannot directly access. In other words, it should take a few days for the money to be transferred if you need access to the funds. This will allow you to think twice before withdrawing your funds and will keep your finances separate. Moreover, this may help curtail any spontaneous purchases, such as a new clothing or the latest techno-gadget. What's more, if you go with an online bank, you will also benefit from slightly better interest rates since their overhead is lower than that of traditional banks.

- Set up a weekly or bi-weekly automatic withdrawal program for a specific amount to be transferred to your savings account. This can be very minimal: $25 per pay period is fine! The goal is to start the habit. It's important to note that this savings account is separate from your retirement savings plan, often a 401(k) in the United States or a Registered Retirement Savings Plan (RRSP) in Canada.

- Make a habit of paying cash for your items and keep the change in a separate jar. Deposit that change at the end of each month in your personal savings account.

- Spend on items that will increase your skills and your net worth, such as education and books. This is good debt because the return on investment is high—your personal growth and development.

- If you spend on bad debt (e.g., electronics, clothes, luxury items), set a budget aside and purchase those items once you have enough money.

- When spending on clothes, buy classic pieces of the best quality you can afford. Take good care of those garments; they will see you through many events and ensure you look good every time. In the long run, you will save money since you will not be replacing your clothes every season.

- Make a habit of having no more than two credit cards: One for regular use with a low interest rate and one for backup or emergencies—preferably with no annual fee and a low interest rate.

- Pay off credit cards each month.

- Give yourself a financial goal. Your goal is highly personal and dependent upon your current financial situation. For example, for some, putting aside $5,000 a year and then investing it may be a difficult, albeit more realistic goal than saving enough for a down payment on a home. Whatever it may be, set a number or other financial goal in your head and go for it!

- Read *Money: Master the Game* by Tony Robbins.

- Read *One-Page Financial Plan* by Carl Richards

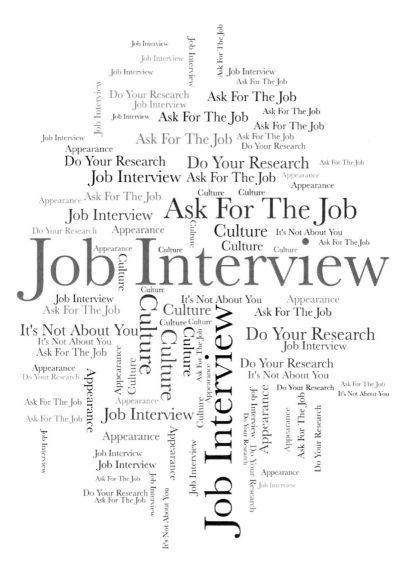

Lesson 6: Know The Anatomy Of The Job Interview

"A job interview is not a test of your knowledge,
but your ability to use it at the right time."

– Anonymous

A job interview is something everyone will have to go through at one point or another. As such, it is also one of the most important professional experiences to master, since you will likely go through several interviews throughout your career. In light of this, this lesson is a bit longer, but well worth the read! In the following pages, I will go through the three components to a job interview—(a) the pre-interview, (b) the interview, and (c) the post-interview—and offer tips and insights to help you get the job you want.

The Pre-Interview

Do Your Research

Congratulations! You've landed an interview! Now is not the time to sit and wait for the big day—you have work to do! If you're applying to an organization you've never worked for before (or even if you are applying for a position in-house), it is critical to research the organization's website. When doing so, look for particular elements, such as the organization's vision and mission, and familiarize yourself with them. Also, find a way of incorporating the organization's philosophy into your responses. Look for key words and find a way of weaving them into your interview. Remember, however, to always be authentic. Make sure that your values align with what you are saying. If not, then why are you there?

Do a quick background check on your potential interview panel. If you don't know who will be interviewing you, run a check on the head of the company, any director that may be your supervisor, as well as the head of human resources. Check for any awards they might have won, articles they may have published, or boards on which they serve. A golden rule to live by is this: When going into a stressful meeting, always know something about your "opponent" or, in this case, the person who may be hiring you. Get to know them <u>virtually</u>; this will give you an advantage and boost your self-confidence going into an interview.

Write Out Possible Interview Questions

To prepare for your meeting, prepare ten to twelve possible interview questions. Then, write down your answers and practice them first out loud, then in front of a mirror, and then with someone. Do this a few weeks before your interview so that the answers roll right off your tongue. Remember to also use the organization's lingo. If you're not sure, look at their website and write down any expressions, project titles, or initiatives that may be in the works and *naturally* plug those into your responses— don't force it. This will undoubtedly catch the panel's attention and they will be more likely to deem you a great fit with the organization's culture.

During the Interview

The First Five Minutes

In her book *I Shouldn't Be Telling You This*, Kate White cites an impressive statistic she found regarding the hiring practices of many reputable organizations: According to the Society for Human Resource Management, 35% of people surveyed said that their decision on whether to hire a candidate or not was made within the <u>first five minutes</u> of the interview! Yikes!

As daunting as this reality may be, it's wise to use this information to your advantage and up your game during these precious initial moments. Here's how:

1. Offer a firm and confident handshake. This will demonstrate confidence, poise, and control—a good start to any interview.

2. Look people in the eye when saying hello and responding to questions. Hold eye contact for a second or two longer. This will signal to the panel that you are in control of the situation and confident with your responses.

3. Mind your posture. Keep your head high and your back straight; don't fidget. When sitting, make sure your tailbone is firmly in contact with the back of the chair. This will automatically straighten posture in your chair.

4. Smile. This helps diminish stress and makes everyone feel at ease.

Your Appearance

I can't stress the importance of making sure your appearance is spot on! This also falls into the "first five minutes" category, but it is so important that I decided to discuss this separately. The following tips apply for regular professional job interviews. Depending on the organizational culture, some suggestions may be ignored. It all depends on your situation. For the following section, however, I am assuming you are interviewing for a fairly conventional, professional setting.

1. Invest in a professional interview outfit, something that will send the following message: "I am professional, competent, and responsible." When in doubt, a simple and professional black dress with a scarf or pin will do wonders and have a positive professional impact.

2. Make sure your clothes are free of stains, pet hair, or lint. This screams sloppy!

3. Style your hair simply. If you normally play with your hair out of nervousness, pull it up away from your face.

4. Keep your makeup simple, fresh, and professional.

5. Hide all tattoos and piercings. Although you may find them stylish and fun, they send out the wrong signal to professional employers. You want the focus to be on you and not your body art.

6. Wear proper shoes. Make sure they are free from scuff marks and that they are subtle and professional. The shoe should be closed toed and not be higher than three inches. Black or neutral colors are best.

Body Language

As previously mentioned in this book, your body language speaks volumes and accounts for up to 55% of your message. Make it count! Here's what you should be looking out for:

1. Keep your head still when talking.

2. Keep both feet on the ground. This signals to the panel that you are, in fact, grounded and are level headed—both literally and figuratively. Avoid at all costs crossing your legs or tucking one of your feet behind your legs. This could signal that you lack confidence and that you are trying to make yourself smaller.

3. Lean in at the table. During the interview, expand your chest and lean in slightly by placing your forearms in front of you and clasping your hands together, signaling to the panel that you are fully present and leaning into the interview with great interest and focus.

It's Not About You

Remember to always <u>focus on the job</u> you're applying for and emphasize <u>what you can offer them to improve their organization.</u> This is so important because they want to see what <u>you</u> can do <u>for them</u>, not what they can do for you. The last thing your interviewer wants to hear is how you were wonderful at your last job and the other personal projects you have on your plate. Always focus your answers on the <u>job you're applying for</u>. Make sure your strengths shine through and align with your place within the organization.

When I went for my first administrative position, I thought I would "wow" my interview panel with facts I learned from my doctoral studies. I stated how I would be an ideal candidate since I was conducting research in my chosen line of work, etc. Well, as it turns out, this only signaled to my panel that I had other major projects on my plate and that I may not be fully invested. You see, they want to feel the love and get all of your attention. Make sure you signal this during your interview—especially at the end. After all, it is about them, not you.

Other Interview Essentials

There are other important factors to keep in mind during the interview.

1. **Be on time.** In fact, arrive 30 minutes prior to your interview. This will give you the chance to warm up, go to the bathroom to practice your power poses (see Lesson 3), get used to the environment, and settle in.

2. **Do not walk into the interview with a coffee.** It signals to the panel that you are taking the interview process too casually. Another factor to keep in mind is that it gives you bad breath and you run the risk of spilling your hot beverage all over the table.

3. **If water is offered, take it**! Unlike coffee, water is acceptable during an interview. It's not uncommon to get a dry mouth during an interview and there's nothing worse than not being able to speak due to this nervous reaction. Just in case, pack a bottle of water in your handbag and have it readily available in case of an emergency.

4. **Have two to three questions ready.** At the end of every interview, you will be asked if you have any questions. Never, ever say no! Always have two to three smart

questions related to the position, written out and ready to be introduced. Focus your questions on your potential new role and make them insightful. Also, ensure that they are properly worded. This is your last chance to make your mark—make it count. When the panel is answering, take down notes, but don't look as if you are evaluating their answers. This is also a great time to connect on a more human level with your panel, since they have a chance to break free from their scripted questions by answering your insightful questions. I remember feelings this when I went into my last interview (and ultimately got the position). I felt that my questions allowed the panel to hone in on their expertise and experiences. I took advantage of this last opportunity to delve into their knowledge and gain valuable insights. It was a nice way to end and made the panel feel good as well.

5. **Ask for the job.** The last thing to do before leaving is to ask for the job! Make one last statement on how you have enjoyed the interview and that you believe your <u>values</u> and <u>work ethic</u> aligns well with those of the organization. Look them in the eye and say that you would love the opportunity to be part of the team and contribute in any way to help promote their vision and mission.

After the Interview

Finally, it's over! You've made it through and you've survived! Now what? A day or two following your interview, send out a personalized letter (e-mail) to each member of the interview panel members thanking them personally for their time and interest in your candidacy. I always like to use a specialized font to make it look like a handwritten note.

Here's what a good thank you letter might look like:

Good afternoon, Mrs. Smith,

Thank you for taking the time to speak with me yesterday about the director's position with Cornerstone Investment, Inc. It was a pleasure meeting with you. Furthermore, I truly enjoyed learning about the company's mission and vision and I believe my leadership style would align well with Cornerstone Investment's future endeavors.

As we discussed, I enjoy both group and independent assignments and I am an early adopter when it comes to innovative practices. I believe these qualities will serve me well in guiding a team toward progress and growth.

I am very excited about the possibility of joining the Cornerstone Investment team and would greatly appreciate a follow-up as you move ahead to the second phase of the hiring process. If you need any further information, please do not hesitate to contact me by e-mail or phone. Thank you for your time and interest in my candidacy.

Best regards,

Daphne Wallbridge

STEP UP DOABLES

- Invest in a great interview outfit (J. Crew, Banana Republic, and Brooks Brothers have beautiful professional suits and dresses for this type of occasion).

- Research the organization you are applying to in order to get a feel for its culture and values.

- Write down and rehearse your interview questions so they become second nature and the words roll right off your tongue.

- Send out a thank you letter a day or two after your interview.

- Make sure all correspondence is free from grammatical and typographical errors. Have someone else read it to make sure.

- Be on time.

- Be yourself and don't forget to smile!

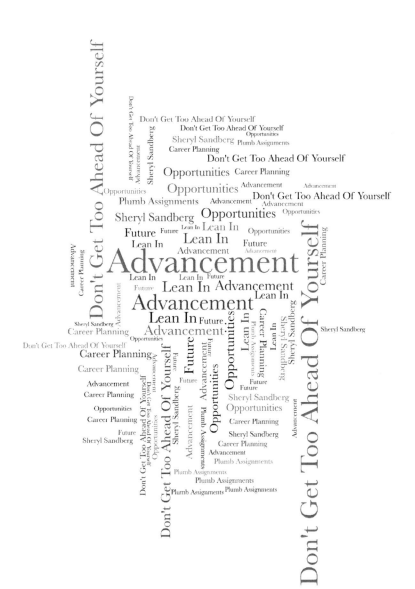

Lesson 7: Don't Get Too Ahead Of Yourself

"Don't enter the workforce already looking for the next exit. Don't put the brakes. Accelerate. Keep a foot on the gas until a decision must be made."

– Sheryl Sandberg, COO of Facebook

Another great piece of advice I read was by Sheryl Sandberg, the author who started it all for me. In her book *Lean In*, Sandberg addresses a phenomenon women often go through called "leaving before you leave." What Sandberg means by this is that women tend to think too far in advance, start planning families and, as a result, "leave" a job before the going gets good. In effect, women tend to forgo any plumb assignments, new challenges, wonderful opportunities for career advancement, and the chance to grow both personally and professionally. In fact, many women look too far down the road and start planning for their future family life—even when they are single—and gradually start putting the brakes on what could be a wonderful career path. Rather than adopting this mindset, Sandberg recommends giving it your all until you are ready to take a break—whether that be to have a child, to go back to school, or to tackle another project. What women need to do is go straight up to the wall and go hard: Ask for challenging, new assignments that will build new critical skills, volunteer to head projects and make presentations, be seen as a "take charge" kind of person, and be there to work with others for the good of the organization. In other words, if you do decide to leave, do so on a high note and make a lasting impression. That way, when you come back, chances are you will be coming back to a career you love and to assignments that mean something to you. In fact, this last point is another good reason to go strong until you leave. The more you do, the more you will be excited to return to work. After a maternity leave, many women look forward to going back to work to engage in adult conversations and tackle new intellectual tasks. Having a thriving and rewarding career to go back to will only help during this transition.

STEP UP DOABLES

- Read *Lean In* by Sheryl Sandberg.
- Make it a habit of being in the moment. Every time you catch yourself thinking too far in advance, stop yourself and focus on what is in front of you. Give it your all and be fully present.
- Make it a habit of volunteering to participate in *selective* new project initiatives at work to continue to build skills and confidence. This will also help you stand out and be seen as a real team player.
- Take advantage of all available networking opportunities, whether during conference lunches, in the elevator, or even at the water cooler. What is important is to be well versed in office small talk and to know the organization's lingo. This will help you create new professional relationships which may serve you well in the future.
- If your boss is at the same conference and there is no formal seating assigned, sit next to her. Not only will this

send a clear message that you are confident, but it will also build your gravitas and offer you valuable airtime with her to get to know her better.

Lesson 8: Know The Difference Between A Mentor And A Sponsor. Have Both.

"Understand that it's not all about you."

– Sylvia Ann Hewlett, Economist

Before I read Sylvia Ann Hewlett's *Forget a Mentor, Find a Sponsor*, I didn't know the difference between a mentor and a sponsor. In fact, I didn't really know sponsors existed. I had heard the term "mentor" and knew it referred to a professional colleague who was higher up in the ranks who was there to guide, support, and offer advice. When I began my career as an educator, I had mentors and sought their advice on a regular basis. I did not discover what a sponsor was, however, until I was entering my second year of doctoral studies. I had just started an educational leadership course, when my professor—who had been impressed with the work I was submitting—asked me if she could chair my dissertation. After that, she put me in contact with other professors from my university and helped me become part of their research hub—something rare for students, since this is a hub devoted to faculty research. Additionally, this professor also asked me to assist her in a large study she was leading within the university's doctoral program. I was so humbled and flattered that she had seen this potential in me that I wanted to make her proud and do my best to assist her in any way I could. This situation is, in fact, what sponsorship is all about: A senior member of your organization sees potential in you and advocates for you to other highly ranked members of the organization. However, sponsorship does not stop there; in fact, it's a two-way street. According to Hewlett, what is important to know about sponsorship is that you also need to give back and keep your sponsor abreast of your progress. After all, you are wearing her *brand* since she did go out on a limb for you. To do right by her, you need to give back, keep the lines of communication open, remain transparent, and look out for her. In other words, the relationship between the sponsor and the sponsored is *reciprocal.*

As you move forward in your career, it's important to keep your eyes open for these people who will come your way. Mentors and sponsors will become key resources as you progress professionally and it's important for you to know the difference between the two. Mentors give advice and offer support; however, they do not have the power to help you move up and promote you for plumb assignments. The relationship is also one way; the mentor works for you to help you navigate your professional environment. A sponsor, on the other hand, has the power to promote you and introduce you to people of power and influence. She will advocate for you, recommend you for challenging and noteworthy assignments, and offer you a protective shield if things go awry. In this relationship, both parties gain from one another and the relationship is more reciprocal. However, it's also important to note that although the sponsored must give back, she will not need to do so *symmetrically.* In other words, the sponsor, who is in a higher position, is there ultimately to elevate the sponsored. The sponsored does not have all the connections and skills the sponsor does. Therefore, to "give back," the sponsored must be grateful, keep her sponsor in the loop, and be willing to keep the communication lines open and honest at all times.

One final note regarding mentors and sponsors. If you are vigilant and mindful, you will be able to gradually find a mentor and naturally develop that working relationship. If you are working in an organization that automatically assigns you one, then that relationship will happen sooner. If not, the process may be longer, though not impossible. Keep an open mind and be ready to approach someone with whom you feel comfortable. This will usually be a relationship that will form with like-minded people that you trust. A sponsor, however, will have to approach you as she sees your potential. This is why networking and making yourself visible through volunteering to do extra projects will go a long way in promoting your potential to future sponsors.

STEP UP DOABLES

- Read *Forget a Mentor, Find a Sponsor* by Sylvia Ann Hewlett.
- Take advantage of all networking opportunities in your organization to see and be seen (see Step Up Doables in Lesson 7).
- Volunteer to help with different assignments and offer to head presentations to keep you in the "spotlight."
- When you find a sponsor, keep the communication lines open, and be transparent and willing to help. Don't forget your sponsor is taking a chance on you and you are wearing her brand; make her proud and go the extra mile.

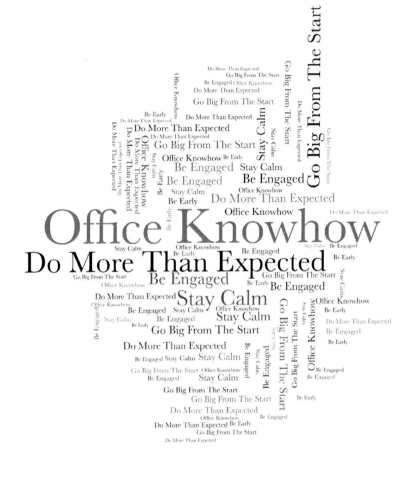

Lesson 9: Learn Office Knowhow

"And as I thought about it, I realized that most of my successes—and the successes of women I knew—always involved going big. Doing a job well is not enough. The key is to do more than what's expected, power it up, go balls to the wall."

– *Kate White, American Author*

Y ou've gone through the interview and you've gotten the job, so now what do you do? One thing is for sure: You need to follow through with what you promised during your interview and start building a solid professional reputation. Here are some key office knowhow tips to remember.

Arrive at Work Before Everyone Else

This is simple and very important. If you're not an early bird, you will be by the time you finish this book. Productivity and great workflow start by embarking on important tasks early on in the morning. You should also approach your career with this philosophy. When you arrive to work before everyone else— preferably one hour or so before—you have the time to boot up your computer, check and respond to some e-mails, clear your desk of any clutter (if it has not been done the night before), and plan and prepare for the upcoming day's work by reviewing your agenda. By adopting this habit, you also have an opportunity to clear your head. This undoubtedly gives you a leg up and gives you a chance to start the day off on the right foot. No matter what comes your way, by arriving to work an hour before your colleagues, you will be poised to tackle any challenges that come your way.

Stay Calm and Carry On

Events will happen and the stress will mount. Whatever happens, do not become frantic and out of control. In other words, whatever the situation, always remain calm, levelheaded, and poised. Think of a duck swimming—calm on the water, but underneath, frantically paddling its way through the current. That can be you. Always appear to be in control. This is not always easy, especially when starting off in a new career, but it is critical to building a solid professional reputation. Remember, nobody wants to work with or for a person who flies off the handle when the going gets tough. To help stay calm and in control, start gathering tricks early on in your career that will help you channel your focus and energy on the task at hand, such as taking a minute to breathe deeply, reviewing the facts, and calling a mentor for guidance. This would also be a good time to use the self-portrait image done in Lesson 1. Remember the tea bag image I conjured up to help me face difficult situations? It works!

Go Big From the Start

Kate White offers another great piece of advice in *I Shouldn't Be Telling You This*: The importance of going big right from the start. In other words, do everything better than expected, go the extra mile, and do so subtly but with energy and enthusiasm. In doing so, this will signal to others—especially your employer— that you are a hard worker, you are able to think outside the box, and you are willing to take on challenging tasks. A good example of this would be in keeping an eye out for what may need fine-tuning around your office and then, bringing it up a notch. If a certain practice seems inefficient, think of a more creative, effective way of addressing it. Your fresh perspective may just be what your organization needs! Moreover, when you have figured out a way of addressing an issue, bring it to your boss's attention and explain why you are doing so. By adopting this practice and professionalism, you will be developing a solid reputation for being a creative problem-solver, looking to increase productivity and ease for everyone. Another great way of going big is to simply do everything as perfectly as you can—without going overboard and reducing productivity, of course. Be meticulous and discerning. Make sure you know which project needs greater attention and prioritize accordingly, respect deadlines by finishing your work a day or two in advance (if possible), pay attention to detail where it counts, and most importantly, keep your boss in the loop with all major changes or possible setbacks.

Avoid Being Part of the Gossiping Tribe

It is easy to get into the habit of talking about others at work. Who doesn't want to partake in a little office gossip after all? The problem is that if you do decide to dish the dirt with the others, you will be guilty by association. What's more, the same people doing it to others will also likely do it to you, and it will show a great lack of professionalism. In fact, it might even undo all the good you are doing within your organization. Remember: Words are powerful and can hurt; therefore, you have a responsibility to use them wisely. What do you do then if you are caught in a situation where people are gossiping? Well, in those situations, it's always better to physically remove yourself. If you can't because it will seem too obvious or uncomfortable, then refuse to speak up on the issue and try and divert the conversation to something more positive. If pressed for your opinion, simply state that you do not know the person that well and don't feel comfortable discussing the issue. Then, steer clear from those gossiping colleagues as much as possible.

Be Fully Engaged

As you move ahead in your career, make sure to also step out of your office and engage the people with whom you will be working. Present yourself, make new acquaintances, and do not be afraid of sharing stories—preferably not work-related. Everyone is human after all and craves authentic human interaction. Offer your <u>authentic self</u> to your new colleagues right from the start. This will signal to them that you are present, ready, and willing to work with them and that you are happy to be part of their team. This is what Sheryl Sandberg did when she first started off as Facebook's COO. She made her way around the office and talked to everyone, introducing herself and delving right into the organizational culture. Her efforts made a good impression from the start. Another point to add is that as you embark on your first days in a new position, don't be afraid to roll up your sleeves and get down to it. In other words, make your mark as soon as possible and dive right in. Not only will this build up your professional status and reputation, but it will also help calm those first-day nerves as you physically engage in the work and make it your own.

STEP UP DOABLES

- Read Kate White's book, *I Shouldn't Be Telling You This.*

- Google Kate White on YouTube and watch some of her talks on managing career life. White's talks are always practical, highly informative, and to the point.

- Have a self-portrait symbol in place to help you navigate stressful situations (see Lesson 1).

- Start waking up an hour earlier to get into the habit of arriving to work earlier. Incidentally, this means going to bed earlier as well.

- Prepare key transition lines to help you get out of sticky situations when you find yourself engaged with gossipers. *Example*: "Sorry to change to subject, but I just remembered an issue I needed your help with. Do you have a minute to lend an ear? I'd love your input on it."

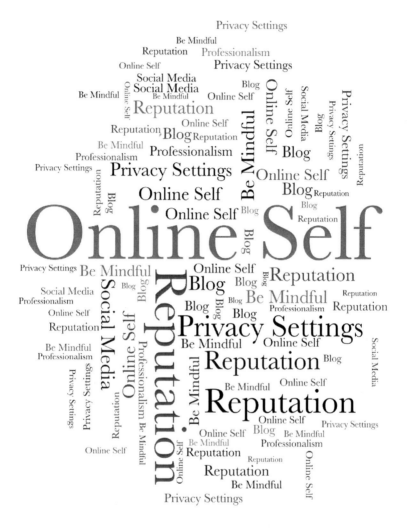

Lesson 10: Mind Your Online Self

"Social networking is a gift economy. The more you participate productively with others, the higher your own profile will be."

– Lois P. Frankel, Author and Executive Coach

Did you know that one of the first things potential employers do nowadays is go online to conduct a search on you? Why is this relevant? Well, it's relevant because in this day and age—where people have gotten into the habit of posting every little detail of their lives online—employers can see for themselves who they may be hiring. Think about it. As an employer, would you be interested in hiring someone who routinely posts photos of herself in a bikini, partying, or getting wasted every weekend? In other words, this due diligence allows potential employers to get to know you quite well—on a more personal level. It also allows them to see for themselves whether or not what they observed during the interview is authentic. If people are not careful and post anything and everything, this will signal to a potential employer that they lack judgment and maturity.

At this point, you may be asking yourself what to do. Should you remove yourself from all social media? Should you drop off from the virtual world all together to make sure your reputation remains intact? Of course not. In fact, having an online presence is critical and can, if used properly, give you a leg up in your career. White and Frankel each provide great tips on how to manage your online presence. Here's what they recommend:

Remove all inappropriate postings from your social media accounts. This would include anything showing partial nudity, alcohol, drugs, violence, as well as other forms of profanity and inappropriate behaviors. In other words, when in doubt, REMOVE.

If you are tagged in any misleading or compromising photos, ask your friend to remove them immediately.

Adjust your privacy settings to make sure you have the utmost control over who sees your content.

Be mindful of who you accept into your online circle. Do you know them? Are they trustworthy? These "friendships" can take on a life of their own, so make sure you check out a potential friend's postings to ensure you really know who they are before accepting them into your circle. If you make a mistake and regret accepting a friend, you can always "unfriend" them. They will not be notified and you will be rid of any potential headaches.

To increase a positive online presence, start a blog related to your profession. This does not have to cost a lot and can become a wonderfully creative outlet where you can display your professional interests. It's also important to keep in mind that the more you post, the more your name will appear under your professional postings. The benefit of this is that it will signal to potential employers that you are not only professional, but also enjoy sharing content and have an interest in self-directed, lifelong learning. Additionally, this is also a great way to push aside any negative online postings that may be difficult to remove since only your new content will find its way to the top.

STEP UP DOABLES

- Do a good clean up of all social media accounts. Remove inactive or potentially "harmful" friends.

- Review privacy settings for all social media accounts and make sure they are set up to give you the most control over your privacy. If you are not certain how to set up proper privacy settings for your social media accounts, do an online search such as, "How do I adjust privacy settings in (name of social media)?" This should yield good results and help you adjust your accounts accordingly.

- Start a professional blog where you share insightful information addressing topics in our field of expertise. If you are just starting off, you can search webhosting services such as Bluehost, eHost, HostClear, iPage, Idea Host, and SiteBuilder. Each of these services will offer what you need to get started and will let you create your own website for a nominal fee, usually somewhere between $2.75 to $3.85 a month.

- If you are going to start a blog, find an online text editor. This will help you ensure that the content you publish has proper grammar and appropriate writing style and has been proofread. To find an editing service that fits your needs, do a basic search and see what comes up.

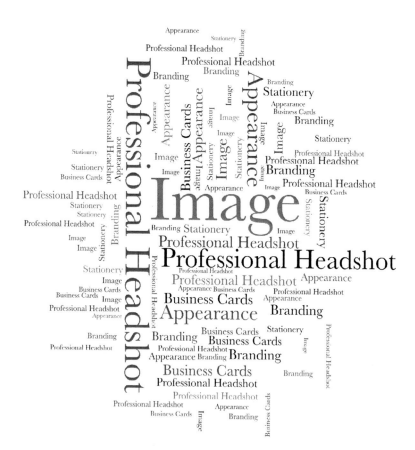

Lesson 11: Invest In Your Image

"The way we dress affects the way we think, the way we
feel, the way we act, and the way others react to us."

– Judith Rasband, American Image Consultant

I remember reading a great consulting book a few years ago by
Elaine Biech called *The Business of Consulting*. In it, Biech often
explained that the way you present yourself to the world—the
way you look, the way you talk, and the quality of the work you
do—directly influence the way people perceive you. As a result,
they will judge you and decide whether or not to hire you. This
might not always be fair, but it's the way life works. However, in
light of this, Biech also recommended investing in yourself—or
your image—to help put yourself in the best light possible. As I
read these passages, I was starting my Step Up blog. Since I was
laying the foundation for future consultant work, I remember
telling myself how correct Biech was, and how important it was
to make sure the message I send out to the world aligns with who
I am and who I ultimately want to be. This is when I decided to
make certain investments. Here's what I did.

Have a Professional Write Your Resume

I collaborated with a firm to create my professional resume.
Not only was this a huge time saver, but it also allowed me to
discuss my accomplishments, goals, and personal qualities that
needed proper highlighting. Once I proofread and approved it,

it was sent to me electronically and I now have it ready to go. Another interesting point is that during my interview with the writer, I was forced to focus on what attributes I had that specifically aligned with the job I wanted. He also found a way to put it all together to truly reflect who I am. Now, all I have to do is adjust it here and there by adding new information every once in a while.

Get a Professional Headshot

People will get a better feel for who you are and as a result, tend to connect with you even more when they have an image of you. That's why it's so important to make the minimal investment (between $100 to $200) of getting a professional headshot taken. Keep it simple and fresh with a neat hair style and makeup applied sparingly. Further, make sure your attire is perfectly tailored and free from any stains. One thing to keep in mind, of course, is that your headshot style will vary according to your profession. Thus, a lawyer and a Broadway actress would not have the same sort of headshot. One will be conservative, while the other more sultry and glamorous. Figure out what your needs are and get that headshot done. Then, post it to your blog.

Have a Web Designer Create Your Blog Page

Although I have mentioned how with the advent of website templates many people are creating their personal blogs, this can become time consuming. As I progressed in my career and as my daughter was getting older, I did not have as much time to fiddle around with plugins and editing options on my website.

Additionally, I wanted my site to stand out and look fresh and professional. I knew that I needed help with this. That's why I decided to invest in professional web design services. Initially, this involved a greater amount of financial resources than I was originally anticipating, but believe me, when you are in the business of consulting, or you are trying to set yourself apart from the competition, having an attractive web page (filled with relevant content) is a feather in your cap. Plus, it attracts more readers. I was fortunate to work with a wonderful group of women at Newbie Media Design. Their approach suited my taste and vision and to this day, I have them work on all marketing aspects of my consulting work. This small initial investment now allows me the freedom to focus on what I love most—creating informative and practical content.

Stationery

Biech also commented on the importance of making sure your stationery—business cards, handouts, and any other paper used—is of the utmost quality. Thus, paying a little more for laser printing, high-quality paper, and professional business cards can go a long way. If necessary, go to a printing shop and have a professional take care of creating and printing your business cards and informative handouts. In doing so, also make sure to use thicker cardstock with a beautiful finish, since this will signal to people that you take pride in your work and offer high-quality, professional services. Doing this will give you a slight psychological advantage.

Your Appearance

I'm sure you've heard the expression, "dress for the job you want." Well, this is true in life in general too. The way you dress, wear your makeup, style your hair, and posture yourself will be important clues to people as to who you are. People judge with their eyes first, so it's important to always put your best foot forward (again, the importance of having a professional head-shot). For example, if you're aspiring toward the next executive position and want to make a good impression, start dressing for it now. If you are in a professional setting, it's best to wear neutral, well-fitted suits or dresses, and keep accessories classic and simple. Make sure your clothing is not too tight (no panty lines or muffin tops showing) and do not show cleavage! Also, keep in mind that many people get turned off with the use of heavy perfumes, so keep it light or avoid it all together. Tattoos and body piercings should be covered. Although they may seem very stylish and a medium for self-expression, they are not appropriate for the formal board room. Know your audience and the work climate, and adhere to it. When in doubt, hide it or don't wear it.

These are only a few recommendations. Depending on your budget and situation, some of the recommendations may be more practical than others. The point is to seek out the help of professionals to get some of the work done—beautifully. When it comes to your image, it's worth the investment since it will bring you peace of mind that you are bringing your best self forward.

STEP UP DOABLES

- Read any book by Nina Garcia on fashion. My favorite is *The One Hundred: A Guide to Pieces Every Stylish Woman Must Own.*

- Do a Google search for local photographers who could do a high-quality headshot.

- Do a Google search of web design/marketing companies who could work with you in creating a beautiful, custom website. If you are lucky, this same business will be able to supply you with stationery options as well (informative pamphlets, business cards, posters).

- Search for a local printing shop where you can have your stationery printed (if not available through your web design company).

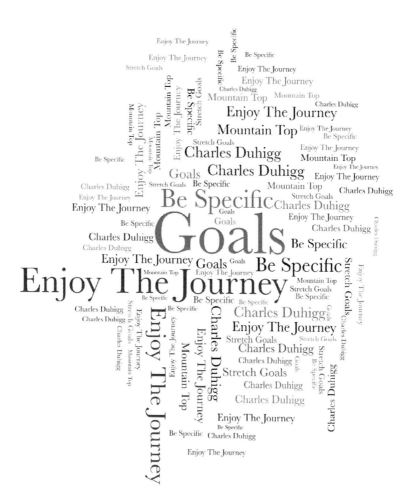

Lesson 12: Set Goals

"What you get by achieving your goals is not as important as what you become by achieving your goals."

– Zig Ziglar, Motivational Speaker

Now, you might be telling yourself that goal setting would be a normal and natural thing to do throughout your career. However, what many people do not know is how to go about doing it to help ensure success while remaining productive and efficient.

It goes without saying that setting goals for ourselves is critical in life and offers us ways of measuring and validating our accomplishments. However, according to Charles Duhigg, (*Smarter, Faster, Better*), there is an art form to setting goals. Duhigg explains that the most productive and successful people start with a vision in mind and then work backwards. Here's how they do it. The first step in setting goals is to imagine your best outcome, your dream come true. This is what Duhigg and many successful CEOs call "stretch goals." Stretch goals are the big final picture you conjure up in your mind, the ideal scenario you want for yourself. This is often a daunting, audacious goal and as a result, it can frighten many people due to its challenging nature. So the question remains: Now that you have an audacious stretch goal written down, what do you do? How do you see it realized? This is where the second part of the equation comes in. According to Duhigg, a stretch goal needs to be combined with several SMART goals. SMART goals are smaller, measurable goals that are easier to achieve in a timely basis. When combining the two—stretch and SMART goals—progress and success naturally occur. Here is an example:

Stretch Goal: To Run a Marathon

SMART Goal

✓ **Specific**: Run 10 km.

✓ **Measurable**: I will train 4 times per week and gradually increase my distance by following my training manual.

✓ **Assignable**: Me (runner), my running friends (training and support).

✓ **Relevant:** Being able to run a 10K is the first step in building my endurance to move ahead and complete a marathon.

✓ **Time-lapsed**: By June 1st.

In this example, I have taken the large goal of completing a marathon and divided it up into smaller steps. Now, as you can see, I start with one SMART goal at a time, or if you prefer, you can include other goals that relate to each SMART goal. For example, for this goal, I could also have a dietary SMART goal or a weight training SMART goal. The point, once again, is to divide the stretch goal up into small, manageable segments that feel doable.

Another important tip on goal setting: It's great that you have goals and that you strive to accomplish them and live your dreams; however, it's also important to review them and check in with yourself. Sometimes we lose our purpose along the way, and the reason we started on our path to attaining our goal. Life happens, goals change, different paths present themselves. This is natural. As CEO of Mohawk Industries, Jeff Lorberbaum, states so well in Jason Jennings's book, *Hit the Ground Running*, "If you're trying to climb one mountain and find that you can't reach the summit, you don't abandon mountain climbing; you change the goal and go for another summit." He goes on to add "Who cares which mountain you climb? The view is great on every mountain" (p. 166). I love that philosophy and find it so liberating! I invite you to keep it in mind as you move forward in anything you do; it will no doubt relieve you of much pressure and aggravation along the way.

STEP UP DOABLES

- Make time every day to think about your dreams. This will allow you the opportunity to play around with different scenarios and get the creativity juices flowing. Journaling is a great way to do this.

- Take a step back once in a while to re-evaluate. Ask yourself if you are still on the right path. If not, adjust and move forward.

- Read the chapter on goal setting in Charles Duhigg's book, *Smarter, Faster, Better*.

- Enjoy the journey!

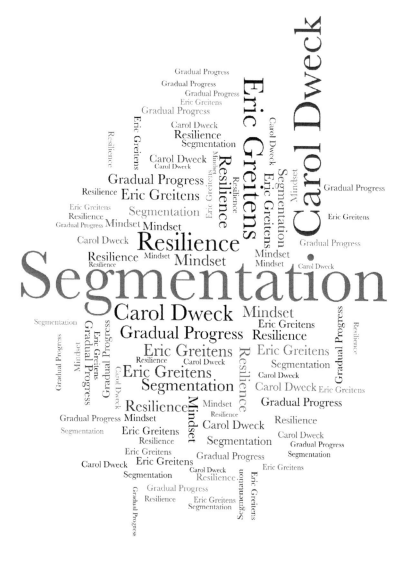

Lesson 13: Practice Segmentation

"You take a number of small steps which you believe are right, thinking maybe tomorrow somebody will treat this as a dangerous provocation. And then you wait. If there is no reaction, you take another step: Courage is only an accumulation of small steps."

– *George Konrad, Hungarian Novelist*

It goes without saying that when you leave your comfort zone, you grow and learn. Carol Dweck, author of *Mindset*, credits her success to this philosophy of pushing one's limits to foster personal growth and inner fulfillment. She calls this adopting a growth mindset. This mindset enables one to focus on the process rather than the end result. It also allows us the freedom to make mistakes without guilt or personal persecution because mistakes are there to help us learn and grow.

As you reflect on this, I invite you to take inventory of your fears. What is stopping you from moving forward? Let me give you an example of what I was of afraid of and how I was able to achieve my goal by tackling my fear 20 minutes at a time.

I remember being afraid of reading Tolstoy's *War and Peace*. I was afraid of starting it because I feared I wouldn't finish it—the sheer length of it paralyzed me. I remember thinking to myself that I would be a failure if I started it and wasn't able to finish it. This fixed mindset (a term also used by Dr. Dweck) had a strong psychological hold that kept me from reading this book. One day, however, I decided to put my fears aside and start reading

War and Peace. I downloaded it to my iPad and set aside 20 minutes a day to read it. Since I already had a routine of walking on the treadmill every morning, I decided to combine the two activities. It took me a year, but I read it. I chipped away at it gradually and finished my project. In the end, consistency and perseverance made it possible.

The practice I adopted to accomplish my goal is what Eric Greitens (*Resilience*) calls "segmentation." Segmentation, in simple terms, is the process of breaking down a large, daunting project into small, manageable segments while remaining focused on the task at hand. The key for me was to schedule it in and be vigilant in respecting my 20 minute "work time." The message here? No matter how big the project or how daunting the task, success will happen by taking small, incremental, and consistent steps.

After completing *War and Peace*, my confidence grew. From there, I read more books and enrolled in professional administrative courses. Each accomplishment was a stepping stone to the next challenge I set for myself. What people often fail to realize is that when you start small, the momentum builds. Today, as people rush around trying to meet deadlines and family responsibilities, it's rare to have time to focus on personal projects. Life is way too crazy for that. So, forget the concept of having a large amount of time blocked off and instead, focus on shorter increments of time to work on your project—20 minutes here and there is a good start. Chip away at it gradually and eventually, you will see that you are accomplishing that goal. Slow and steady will win this race!

STEP UP DOABLES

- Figure out what you want to accomplish (see Lesson 12 on goal setting). This can be a good journaling exercise.

- Set aside 20 minutes a day to devote to your project. Remember to get creative. Your 20 minutes can be used during your commute to work or while you wait for an appointment. Book it in your calendar—what gets marked down, gets done!

- If you are having difficulty carving out 20 minutes during your day, do a daily activity inventory for a couple of days. Write down what you do and for how long—be honest! When you go over your activities, look for pockets of time that you could have been spending on your project. Social media, texting, or watching television are often major time wasters.

- Plan ahead and be ready. You know what your day will be like, and you will also likely know the times when you will have 20 minutes to focus on your project. Have your tools (e.g., books, notes, and technology) nearby. Maximize every minute you have. In the end, those minutes add up.

- Take stock. Once a week, look at what you've accomplished and celebrate! Journal about your progress or share it with a friend. By having your work validated, you will feel motivated to keep moving forward, thus fostering a growth mindset.

- If you are still having difficulty finding time to work on your project, wake up earlier. That always works!

- Watch Eric Greitens's 3-minute video entitled *How to Deal With Difficult Situations*.

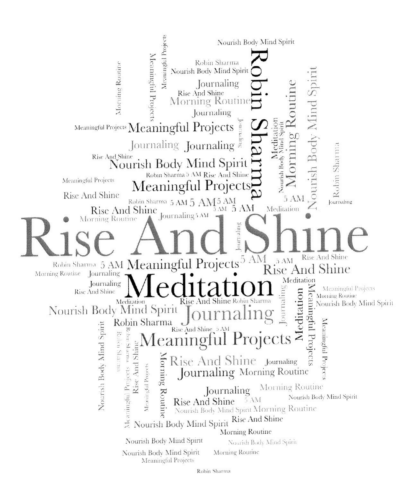

Lesson 14: Rise And Shine

"It is well to be up before daybreak, for such habits contribute to health, wealth, and wisdom."

– *Aristotle, Greek Philosopher*

Although we all have 24 hours in a day, it seems that some people are able to use those hours more efficiently than others. Why is that and, more importantly, *how* to they do it? I'm sure you've heard of Benjamin Franklin's expression, "When you want something done, ask a busy person." No words have ever been truer.

Robin Sharma addresses this concept in *The Monk Who Sold His Ferrari*, which, incidentally is a fabulous read and a great help to redirect your life toward a more meaningful path. In the book, Sharma discusses the importance of getting up early and recommends waking up at 5 a.m. every weekday to get a jumpstart to your day. Yes, you read that correctly: 5 a.m.! Even though this may seem very early for many, the benefits of waking up at 5 a.m. far outweigh the challenges of getting out of bed. In fact, this healthy ritual will allow you to capture precious time to properly exercise, gather your thoughts, plan your day, set or review goals, and get important work done—all before 6 a.m. What's more, you'll also feel more energized because you will have taken control over your day and made time for yourself.

This is an important lesson because by starting this early morning wake-up ritual at the beginning of your career, you will be setting yourself up with the time you need to address what is important to you—your mind, soul, body, and spirit. Furthermore, as time passes and your home responsibilities continue to increase, it will get more difficult to carve out any time to work on yourself and regenerate. Thus, if you are already in the habit of rising and shining at the crack of dawn, you will be more likely to find balance and well-being as you progress in your career.

The following table displays an example of a morning routine. Notice how it incorporates the essentials—mind, body, spirit.

5:00 a.m. to 5:05 a.m.	Meditation/visualization
5:05 a.m. to 5:15 a.m.	Journaling: set goals, write out what you are grateful for, comment on your feelings, frustration, dreams, etc.
5:15 a.m. to 5:30 a.m.	Learn: Read a book chapter, an interesting article, etc.
5:30 a.m. to 6:00 a.m.	Exercise: Walk, stretch, lift light weights, etc.

Now, this is just an example. Some people may wish to focus more on learning, while others on visualization. It all depends on your interests and preferences. I love exercising while reading or listening to an audiobook. That means I can carve out more time for meditation or journaling. If you get resourceful, you can undoubtedly find creative ways of combining activities to maximize your time. What's key is to make sure you focus on the three pillars of a good morning routine—mind (learning), body (exercise), and spirit (meditation/visualization).

STEP UP DOABLES

- Go to bed at a reasonable time to make sure you get between 7 and 8 hours of sleep.

- Start slowly. During the first week of your new morning regime, set your alarm clock 15 minutes earlier than you would normally and incrementally work your way toward waking up at 5 a.m. That way, you will be gradually training yourself to wake up earlier every day.

- When your alarm clock goes off, get up right away. DO NOT hit the snooze button, as you will be defeating the purpose. In fact, you may want to place your alarm clock across the room to help ensure that you get out of bed to shut it off.

- Before going to bed, make sure to organize what you want to work on the next morning. This will save you time and allow you to get started right away. In other words, set up your work station—whatever it may be.

- Read Robin Sharma's book, *The Monk Who Sold His Ferrari*.

- Watch Robin Sharma's video entitled, *How to Wake Up Early*.

Lesson 15: Learn To Embrace Change

"Change can be scary, but you know what's scarier? Allowing fear to stop you from growing, evolving, and progressing."

– Mandy Hale, American Author

As you move forward in your career, you will undoubtedly experience change. This change can be brought on by a move, a change of profession, issues related to aging, ascending the career ladder, or even a change in relationships. No matter the cause, change is never easy. Robin Sharma, a leadership expert and inspirational speaker, often explains in his instructional videos and books that change is frightening in the beginning, messy in the middle, and glorious in the end. In my experience, that about sums it up! However, that simple formula helps us accept what I call the life cycle of change. When we see change through this perspective, it makes the process much more pleasant. Simply put, we are able to be more at ease with what we're feeling when we are aware of the cycle.

Furthermore, in her book *I Shouldn't Be Telling You This*, Kate White explains that once change has occurred and you are trying to start off on the right foot (especially in a new position), it's critical to either go big or go home. In other words, put 110% into everything you do, especially in the beginning when you're trying to make the best impression. It's the best way to hit the ground running and build the confidence you need to push through the challenges brought forth by your new situation. White does caution, however, that not everyone may be on board with your enthusiasm. In fact, some may wish that you would go home instead of going big. This may be because deep down, they feel threatened, inconvenienced, jealous, or even resentful. Under those circumstances, it's important to recognize this, but continue to stay true to your course. Embrace your new challenges, enjoy the process, and go for it!

Three Tips on Going BIG When Embracing Change

Show up at work before everyone else. This gives you the chance to review your messages, organize your to-do list, and set priorities—key in being and feeling in control.

Try solving a recurring problem. Get creative. Sometimes even making slight adjustments can make a world of difference. For example, if people are constantly complaining about performance being down in November, examine the numbers or observe others' behaviors during those times, and do the research. You may discover that those particular times of the year are when people feel discouraged due to the weather getting colder and days beginning to shorten. As such, you may want to organize a social event to help boost morale, or look into lunchtime yoga or meditation classes for employees. In other words, you may wish to find a stress relief outlet that can re-energize and keep the team productive during those key months.

When handing in a report or assignment, make extra notes and offer personal insights. Offer sound suggestions and try to come up with a new thought-provoking idea. To do this, make sure you have the necessary data and strong, factual arguments. Not only will this be a great service to your boss, but this will also display your sense of initiative and willingness to be a team player.

Accept that change will be messy and uncomfortable, but that in the end, it will be well worth the sacrifice.

STEP UP DOABLES

- Watch Robin Sharma's video entitled *The Princess + the Bentley*. It can be found with a simple Google search.

- When contemplating change, list all the "pros" and "cons" and evaluate whether the change is necessary. Often it is. If so, do it.

- Adopt Tina Fey's philosophy: "Say yes, and figure it out later!"

- Remain positive during the process.

- Journal your thoughts onto paper as you undergo change. Later on, you will be amazed to see how you coped with the change and what tools you used to push through.

- Remember that you are not alone. Ask for help.

- Ask for feedback, graciously accept it, and see it as a gift.

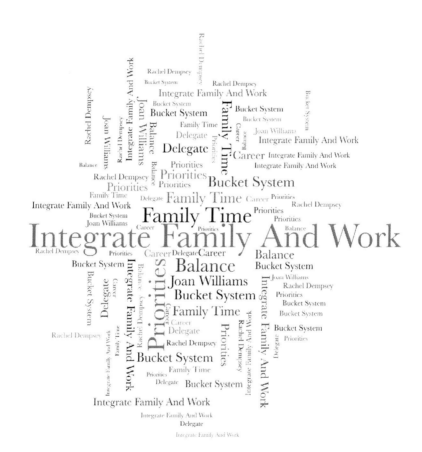

Lesson 16: Know How To Integrate Family And Work

"I have so much admiration for women who are
mothers, who balance family and work."

– Beyoncé, Singer

Whether you are starting off your career as a single woman or are in the middle of your career with a family and hoping to move up the professional ladder, there comes a time where one must juggle both her personal and professional life in order to stay sane.

At a time when technology is at our fingertips, many busy career women may feel overwhelmed that they cannot completely detach themselves from the office. Although the convenience of smartphones and other devices has made facetime in the work setting less demanding, these devices are often the reason that work seeps into family or personal time. What's more, children may feel that mom is there physically, but not really "there" emotionally, given her divided attention.

This reality is becoming increasingly common for many career women and is worth mentioning to the younger generation of professional women. As such, the purpose of this lesson is to rethink work–life balance and set clear boundaries that you and your family will embrace. After all, work is not going away (unless, of course, you win next week's Super Lotto!).

It's no secret that many women feel guilty when they hear comments from others (usually other women) regarding their absence at a child's function or about long hours at the office. Given the unique challenges working mothers face, Joan Williams and her daughter Rachel Dempsey, authors of *What Works for Women at Work*, offer some sage and practical advice on managing career and motherhood.

STEP UP DOABLES

- Make standing lunch dates with your children once or twice a week. Book them in your calendar and stick to them. You can pass them off as "meetings." Depending on your work setting, this can be at your discretion. An added bonus of these lunch dates is that they help make up "family time" when some work projects demand longer hours.

- At the beginning of every semester, take time to ask your children which three of four events they would really like you to attend. Then, mark those events down in your calendar and respect those dates—no matter what. By doing this, it signals to your children that you value them and their activities, that they are a priority to you, and that you want to be involved in their lives.

- As an added bonus, pop in on one or two of your children's other activities. If they're not aware that you will be attending, this surprise visit will be an extra treat.

- Create a "bucket" system to organize your family's duties:
  1. Essentials: talent shows, recitals, soccer games;

2. Take turns: appointments, school fundraisers; and

3. Delegables: errands like picking up dog food or phar-macy runs.

- Read *What Works for Women at Work* by Joan Williams and Rachel Dempsey.

- Lastly, Williams and Dempsey stress the importance of always leaving home with a smile and returning home with a smile. This signals to your children that everything is okay, that mom is happy working, and that she is also happy to return home. In doing so, we are being positive role models for our children, especially our daughters.

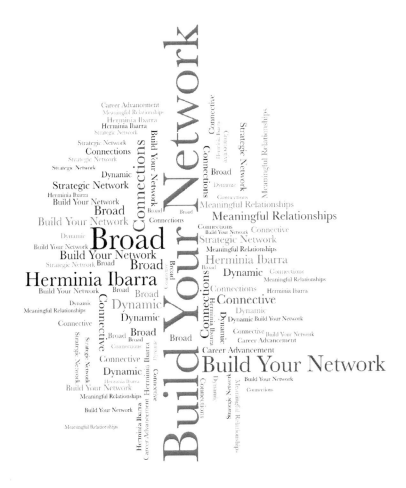

Lesson 17: Build Your Network

> "The richest people in the world look for and build
> networks. Everyone else looks for a job."
>
> *– Robert Kiyosaki, American Businessman*

For many women, the idea of networking can make them cringe. In fact, according to Johanna Barsh, author of *How Remarkable Women Lead*, and Herminia Ibarra, professor of organizational behavior at INSEAD, women view people who network as pushy, inauthentic, and communicating under contrived circumstances. In fact, because so many women fall into the role of nurturers and caregivers, they see networking as an awkward fit as it promotes aggressiveness. Barsh adds that men, on the other hand, see themselves as hunters and ambitious leaders. As such, networking is considered a necessary skill which must be honed to ensure professional survival.

Because of this disconnect, women push away any thought of networking because it conflicts with their family and household responsibilities. In fact, Sheryl Sandberg points out in her book, *Lean In*, that when both husband and wife are employed full time, the women still absorb 40% more of the childcare responsibilities and 30% more housework. Men, on the other hand, are usually willing to stay longer after work and connect, network, and have drinks with team members or clients. For men, as Sandberg point out, this after-hours connection is an extension of their workday and helps them close deals and push projects forward. Lastly, while women often feel they do not have enough energy or time to devote to cultivating lasting and meaningful relationships, men, conversely, are happy with the casual and light "connections" which help their advancement in the long run.

This is where the difference lies: In the definition of networking. For women, networking means developing meaningful relationships; for men, networking means making exciting and profitable connections. See the difference? Which one do you think is more profitable in the professional world?

When assessing the benefits men reap through their connections, it's clear to see that networking is NOT optional. If you want to be an agent of change, to make a difference and to feel like you are part of a team, you need to network—simple as that. The sooner you accept this and actively partake in building your network, the better.

However, building a network is an art. In essence, this means having a varied and balanced group of people in your circle. In that circle, keep your network authentic and only include people you highly respect. These people can be clients, customers, colleagues, administrators, mentors, and professors. To this end, Ibarra explains that there are three forms of networks: (a) an operational network, consisting of professional colleagues from your immediate work environment; (b) a personal network, which is discretionary and consists of family members and friends; and (c) a strategic network, which consists of people from varied backgrounds that serve as connectors and links to extend your current network. Strategic networks are the most critical for career advancement since they, in fact, allow you to branch out and gain greater exposure in your career. For strategic networks to be effective, Ibarra states that they should consist of three qualities; they should be <u>broad, connective, and dynamic</u>. In other words, strategic networks should be cross-cultural, they should consist of people at various professional levels which go beyond your immediate professional circle, and they should be continuously growing.

STEP UP DOABLES

- Read *How Remarkable Women Lead* by Johanna Barsh, Susie Cranston, and Geoffrey Lewis.

- Read *Act Like a Leader, Think Like a Leader* by Herminia Ibarra.

- Watch Building Effective Networks in the *Lean In* educational videos series.

- Make a list of current professional and personal contacts and make sure there is room on your page for new entries.

- Set aside time every week (20 minutes will do) to reach out to a member of your network. Mark this in your calendar when you are planning out your week. This can be done by sending a quick e-mail or calling to check in. You may want to share an article you think may be of interest, or give her a tip on an upcoming conference you think she might want to attend.

- Attend professional conferences and give yourself a goal to meet at least four people. When doing so, don't forget to exchange business cards. Then, a few weeks later, reach out to those contacts to tell them how much you enjoyed talking with them. Make sure to add something personal from your conversation to make the person feel unique and valued. This will go a long way in building your network and undoubtedly, you will make friends along the way. Example: *I really enjoyed meeting you at the Cornerstone Investment conference last week. I remember you telling me you enjoyed photography. I wanted to let you know that there will be a photography exhibit in New York in three weeks. I have attached more information on the event in case you wanted to attend.*

- Make sure you network with your day-to-day colleagues as well. The aforementioned technique is also very important to use with the people you see every day. It will signal to them that you pay attention and that you care—very important in boosting your likability quotient.

Lesson 18: Embrace Feedback

"Feedback is a free education to excellence. Seek it with sincerity and receive it with grace."

– Ann Marie Houghtailing, Founder of Millionaire Girls' Movement

I know that for many of us, the idea of receiving feedback makes us very nervous. This is understandable, as many of us see and hear of feedback in a negative light. The issue we often have with feedback is that we can feel personally criticized when it is being given to us. It's almost as though our character is being targeted, but in fact, that's not at all what feedback is about. Rather, constructive feedback is about honing in on what needs attention professionally or skill-wise, to help you move forward and be successful. It's about helping you develop to ultimately become the best professional you! Kim Ward Gaffney, coaching leader at Pricewaterhouse Coopers (PwC) and Michael Fenlon, Global talent leader at PwC, explain that feedback should be seen as a gift and a tool for personal and professional growth. To help further understand this concept of growth through feedback, Gaffney and Fenlon recommend focusing on the acronym AWARE. Here's how:

A Ask for feedback. This is critical. Be the first to take action by seeking valuable, growth-oriented feedback. Ask your boss, your colleagues, and your friends.

W Watch out for emotions. Receiving feedback can at times be frustrating, stressful, and challenging. When this happens and you feel that emotions are intensifying, it's always best to take a pause and recalibrate. Simply ask for a minute to regroup and take a breath. There is no use continuing a conversation when you are emotionally non-receptive.

A Ask for specifics. Get examples of when you have displayed a certain behavior. This will help you understand where the feedback is coming from. This will also enhance your awareness of your actions and words, and ultimately help improve your overall performance since you will know what to look out for and correct.

R Reach out for perspectives. Discuss your feedback with trusted friends and colleagues and ask them for their input. This will help you gain a better understanding of what you need to work on in a supportive, non-hostile setting.

E Engage your potential. Remember that feedback is not personal; it's about improvement and growth. Take time to thoroughly evaluate the feedback given, adopt a growth mindset, and dive in!

STEP UP DOABLES

- Watch the video Focusing on Feedback in the Leanin.org education section
- Read *Mindset* by Carol Dweck to fully understand the power of growth mindsets—an essential element in accepting feedback.
- Be proactive. Set up regular feedback meetings with your superior where you can address anything that needs focus. Arrive with a positive attitude and remember that these

sessions are to ensure your growth and progress. These meetings are especially important when starting a new position or heading a new initiative.

Lesson 19: Build Your Library, Grow Your Mind

"Ordinary people have big TVs, extraordinary people have big libraries."

— Robin Sharma, Canadian Self-Help Author and Leadership Speaker

This last lesson is my favorite. Throughout the years, I must have read hundreds of books and articles on leadership, management, empowerment, communication, and the like. All of these works have positively impacted both my personal and professional lives. Every time I finish reading a book or watching an inspiring TED talk, I always feel energized and filled to the brim with confidence and enthusiasm. It's quite addictive, actually! One of the first books I read in the beginning of my empowerment/leadership journey was *Think and Grow Rich* by Napoleon Hill, the original guru of self-improvement and leadership. This was a substantial work and possessed at its core all of the essential elements that I would eventually come across in my other readings. Throughout his lessons, Hill often discussed the importance of self-cultivation through education. By "education," Hill was adamant that learning could be accomplished through readings, observations, and life experience. This dictum really resonated with me, as I derive a tremendous amount of pleasure and energy through my readings and, therefore, could relate to what Hill was saying. From that moment on, I canceled my cable subscription and spent my free time reading and developing myself. This was an incredible feeling because it gave me full freedom and control over my thoughts. I was constantly developing my mind, my creativity, and exploring different avenues I never thought possible. I felt alive. This was especially important since as a new mother, I was also struggling to regain some form of control and independence without feeling guilty. My books offered me refuge from the day-to-day mundane chores and allowed me to adopt a healthy growth mindset.

So, dear reader, for this last lesson, I encourage you to build your library! Stock it to the brim with all sorts of wonderful books. Find time each and every day to step away from the mayhem to feed that wonderful mind of yours! To offer some inspiration, I am providing a list of influential and inspirational books and talks that have impacted me, transformed me, and acted as my personal board of directors and coaches along my professional journey.

STEP UP DOABLES

- Sign up for an Audible audiobooks account. This is a wonderful resource that allows you to "read" inspiring and insightful books while on the road or when working out! The relationship you develop with the narrator also adds to the experience. An added bonus is that you can book-mark sections of the audiobook for quick reference.

- Download books on an iPad or another digital reading device. I know some of you are still purists when it comes to reading "real" books, but the convenience of having an entire library in your handbag also has its advantages. One great feature e-books have is the built-in "search" option. This makes retrieving key information quick and easy.

- Get a library card. Libraries offer such a wide array of books and resources. There is something so relaxing and soothing in taking the time to read in a library. It's as though you step away from the white noise to feed your mind and soul. Make sure to make good use of your local library.

- When reading a book, write down any books referenced by the author. Chances are you will also enjoy them, since they will likely align with your interests. This is a great way to expand your library and get to know the specialists in your field of interest.

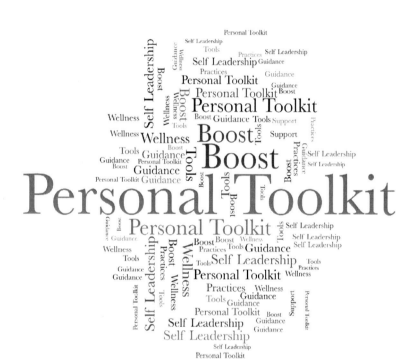

Lesson 20: Learn To Build Your Personal Toolkit

"I wanted to be emotionally self-sufficient, so I didn't depend on other people or circumstances to boost me up, and didn't let them drag me down."

– *Gretchen Rubin, American Author*

Let's face it. Life can be challenging and difficult at times. You feel pulled in every direction with your career, family responsibilities, and other relationships and tasks. It's easy to become overwhelmed and stressed out. What's more, you don't want these feelings taking over your life and diminishing its quality, especially when you should be thriving, experiencing wonderful new challenges, and growing. As such, it's also important to develop and build your personal toolkit. A personal toolkit is a collection of strategies and resources you can easily access and keep nearby to help you navigate challenging times. Their main purpose is to help you channel your energy productively and help you stay on course. Your tools can come in the form of books, productivity apps, practices, and rituals. Here's what I keep in my toolkit.

✓ A well-stocked virtual and physical library: I refer to my books regularly. I have a physical library of my favorite books in my office. They offer me support, guidance, and comfort.

✓ A family photo "shrine" in my office to help me be grateful: When times are stressful, or when I want to take a break, I love looking at the beautiful faces of my husband and daughter. Just seeing them reminds me of how fortunate I am to be sharing a life with them.

✓ Daily meditation practices: I have an application on my iPhone, iPad, and computer called "OMG. I Can Meditate!" It's wonderful and offers hundreds of different meditations. When I only have 10 minutes, I do a shorter meditation; at night, I indulge in a longer bedtime one. Meditation practice has improved my focus and overall sense of well-being.

✓ Daily walking: Not only is walking good for my health, but done early in the morning, it also boosts my endorphins and helps me clear my head. I feel focused, energized, and ready to take on my day as soon as I step off the treadmill.

✓ My Audible account: I can't say enough about audiobooks! What a wonderful way to gain knowledge and fill your time—especially when exercising, driving to work, or puttering around the house! It's worth getting the monthly subscription to take advantage of their great deals as well!

✓ My virtual journal: As I've mentioned throughout the book, I keep a journal. In it I write down my thoughts, dreams, goals, and plans. I find that the practice of journaling every day helps me stay focused and grounded. It also allows me to pour onto "virtual paper" the white noise that could be cluttering my mind. A great way to relieve stress.

✓ My Moleskine notebook: I carry my notebook with me everywhere I go. In it, I take down important information that might come my way, and I post article clippings or other information that I don't want to lose.

✓ My laptop: This is my main creative tool. I write everything in it. I create books, photo albums, blog, connect, and lose myself in my computer.

✓ My Step Up blog: I love my blog (www.stepuplcg.com) because it allows me to channel my creative energy productively. I can easily lose myself when writing, especially when it relates to a subject I am passionate about, such as women's leadership issues. I love posting in it and sharing content with my readers. I see this as my tool for helping women live their best lives and for me, that is pure happiness.

✓ My Fitbit: This little device is key in helping me stay fit and active. I get such an energy boost when I feel it buzz, letting me know that I've achieved my daily goal of walking 12,000 steps!

✓ A small water fountain

✓ Relaxing piano music

So, there you have it. So far, these are the tools I keep nearby to help me along my journey. Each one of you will have different tools according to your needs and realities. What's most important is to start building that toolkit now and to keep adding to it. As time moves on, you will keep going back to those tools. They will see you through your most challenging times and help you grow along the way.

STEP UP DOABLES

- Do some soul searching to find out what tools, rituals, or activities you constantly go to during challenging times.

- Make a list of these items or activities and keep the list close by so you can refer to them when needed.

- Constantly seek new tools, rituals, or activities that will strengthen you. Add them to your daily routine and toolkit.

- Don't wait for a crisis to implement these tools. Use them on a regular basis to help you build strength and resilience. Then, when times get tough, you will have already established a healthy habit of taping into your personal toolkit.

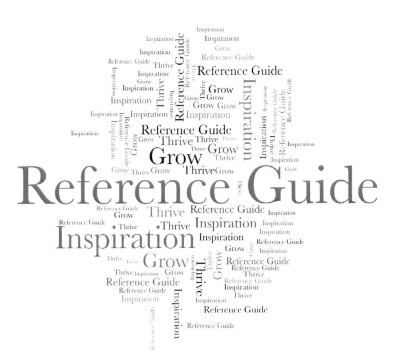

Bonus Lesson

This last "lesson" is meant to be a reference guide to books and talks that have served me well throughout my life, and whose messages have inspired me to act, grow, and thrive both professionally and personally. I hope you enjoy them as much as I have!

STEP UP DOABLES

Suggested Readings and Videos

- Amuroso, S. (2015). *#Girlboss*. New York, NY: Penguin.

- Anderson, C. J. (2016). *TED talks: The official TED guide to public speaking*. Toronto, ON: Harper Collins.

- Buckingham, M. (2009). *Find your strongest life: What the happiest and most successful women do differently*. Nashville, PA: Nelson.

- Cain, S. (TED). (n.d.). *The power of introverts* [Video file]. Retrieved from http://leanin.org/education/ted-talk-the-power-of-introverts/

- Catmull, E. (2014). *Creativity, Inc.: Overcoming the unseen forces that stand in the way of true inspiration*. Toronto, Canada: Random House.

- Duckworth, A. (2016). *Grit: The power of passion and perseverance*. Toronto, ON: Harper Collins.

- Grant, A. [TED]. (n.d.). *The surprising habits of original thinkers* [Video file]. Retrieved from http://leanin.org/education/the-surprising-habits-of-original-thinkers/

- Huffington, A. (2014). *Thrive: The third metric to redefining success and creating a life of well-being, wisdom, and wonder.* New York, NY: Harmony.

- Ibarra, H. (2015). *Think like a leader, act like a leader.* Boston, MA: Harvard Business School.

- Kay, K., & Shipman, C. (2014). *The confidence code.* New York, NY: Harper Collins.

- Kruse, K. (2015). *15 secrets successful people know about time management.* Philadelphia, PA: Kruse Group.

- Rubin, G. (2009). *The happiness project.* New York, NY: Harper Collins.

- Rubin, G. (2012). *Happier at home.* Toronto, Canada: Doubleday.

- Sandberg, S. (2013). *Lean in for graduates.* New York, NY: Random House.

- Sharma, R. (1999). *The monk who sold his Ferrari.* Toronto, Canada: Harper Collins.

- Sharma, R. (2010, June 4). *Robin Sharma - 5 tips on how to wake up early* [Video file]. Retrieved from https://www.youtube.com/watch?v=z6hsOLVwfFc

- Sinek, S. (2009). *Start with why: How great leaders inspire everyone to act.* New York, NY: Penguin.

- Sinek, S. (2014). *Leaders eat last: Why some teams pull together and others don't.* New York, NY: Penguin.

- Thomas, G. [IN]. (n.d.). *How to manage your inner critic.* [Video file]. Retrieved from http://leanin.org/education/how-to-manage-your-inner-critic/

Conclusion

It is an exciting time to be a woman, whether you are starting off in your career, or you are mid-career, looking for new challenges and opportunities. Whatever the case may be, there are so many possibilities and options available out there. In this book, I've tried to touch on the key lessons that I believe are critical to either getting a proper "jump start," or to boosting one's career. In other words, the roadmap is set out, so to speak. Now, it's up to you to keep finding your way and discovering who you are and shaping who you will become. My hope is that this book will act as a practical resource guide and be referenced when needed. It's my way of being there for you when you need me. At some time in your life, you may need one lesson more than another and that's okay. The point is that this book is meant to offer simple but sound advice that can help you step up and step out in confidence, knowing that you have everything in you to take on any new challenge. Until then, I wish to leave you with these final thoughts.

- ✓ Never stop reaching.
- ✓ Stay focused on what matters most to you—Your values, your purpose, your passion, your WHY.
- ✓ Take the time to pause and reflect on the journey you are on. If need be, realign to stay on track.
- ✓ Have faith in your abilities and your strengths by gravitating toward activities that energize and inspire you.

✓ Never, ever stop learning and growing—embrace life-long learning.

✓ Each day, strive to challenge yourself through incremental, small steps.

✓ Develop healthy habits (it's the key to building resilience and developing grit).

✓ Take time to savor the process and enjoy your transformation.

References

Alter, C. H. (2012). *The credibility code: How to project confidence and competence when it matters most.* USA: Meritus Books.

Barsh, J., Cranston, S., & Lewis, J. (2009). *How remarkable women lead: The breakthrough model of work and life.* New York, NY: Crown Business.

Beers, C. (2012). *I'd rather be in charge: A legendary business leader's roadmap for achieving pride, power and joy at work.* New York, NY: Vanguard Press.

Biech, E. (2007). *The business of consulting: The basics and beyond* (2nd ed.). San Francisco, CA: Pfeiffer.

Cuddy, A. (TED). (2012). *Amy Cuddy: Your body language shapes who you are* [Video file]. Retrieved from https://www.ted.com/talks/amy_cuddy_your_body_language_shapes_who_you are

Cuddy, A. (2015). *Presence: Bringing your boldest self to your biggest challenges.* New York, NY: Hachette Book Group.

Cuddy, A. J., Wilmuth, C. A., Yap, A. J., & Carney, D. R. (2015). Preparatory power posing affects nonverbal presence and job interview performance. *Journal of Applied Psychology, 100,* 1286–1295. doi:10.1037/a0038543

Duhigg, C. (2016). *Smarter faster better: The secrets of being productive in life and business.* Toronto, Canada: Doubleday.

Dweck, C. (2008). *Mindset: The new psychology of success.* New York, NY: Random House.

Frankel, L. P. (2007). *See Jane Lead*. New York, NY: Hachette Book Group.

Frankel, L. P. (2014). *Nice girls don't get the corner office* (2nd ed.). New York, NY: Hachette Book Group.

Friedman, S. D. (2014). *Leading the life you want: Skills for integrating work and life*. Boston, MA: Harvard Business School Publishing.

Garcia, N. (2010). *The one hundred: A guide to pieces every stylish woman must own*. New York, NY: It Books.

Greitens, E. (2015, March 25). *How to Deal with Difficult Situations from Eric Greitens' Resilience audiobook* [Video file]. Retrieved from https://www.youtube.com/watch?v=7VV5_MhD030

Gruenfeld, D. [Lean In]. (n.d.). *Power and influence* [Video file]. Retrieved from http://leanin.org/education/power-influence/

Hewlett, S. A. (2013). *Forget a mentor, find a sponsor*. New York, NY: Harvard Business School Publishing.

Hewlett, S. A. (2014). *Executive presence*. New York, NY: Harper Collins.

Hill, N. (2005). *Think and grow rich*. New York, NY: Penguin.

Ibarra, H. (2015). *Think like a leader, act like a leader*. Boston, MA: Harvard Business School.

Ibarra, H. [IN]. (n.d.). *Building effective networks* [Video file]. Retrieved from http://leanin.org/education/building-effective-networks/

Jennings, J. (2009). *Hit the ground running*. New York, NY: Penguin.

Richards, C. (2015). *The one-page financial plan: A simple way to be smart about your money*. New York, NY: Portfolio.

Robbins, T. (2014). *Money: Master the game*. New York, NY: Simon & Schuster.

Sandberg, S. (2013). *Lean in: Women, work and the will to lead*. New York, NY: Random House.

Tolstoy, L. (2008). *War and peace*. New York, NY: Random House.

White, K. (2012). *I shouldn't be telling you this*. New York, NY: Harper Collins.

Williams, J. C., & Dempsey, R. (2014). *What works for women at work: Four patterns working women need to know*. New York, NY: New York University Press.